# Be a Dividend
# Millionaire

# Be a Dividend Millionaire

*A Proven, Low-Risk Approach That Will Generate Income for the Long Term*

Paul Rubillo

Vice President, Publisher: Tim Moore
Associate Publisher and Director of Marketing: Amy Neidlinger
Executive Editor: Jeanne Glasser
Editorial Assistant: Pamela Boland
Operations Manager: Gina Kanouse
Senior Marketing Manager: Julie Phifer
Publicity Manager: Laura Czaja
Assistant Marketing Manager: Megan Colvin
Cover Designer: Alan Clements
Managing Editor: Kristy Hart
Project Editor: Jovana San Nicolas-Shirley
Copy Editor: Apostrophe Editing Services
Proofreader: Sheri Cain
Indexer: Angela Martin
Senior Compositor: Gloria Schurick
Manufacturing Buyer: Dan Uhrig

© 2011 by Paul Rubillo
Publishing as FT Press
Upper Saddle River, New Jersey 07458

**This book is sold with the understanding that neither the author nor the publisher is engaged in rendering legal, accounting, or other professional services or advice by publishing this book. Each individual situation is unique. Thus, if legal or financial advice or other expert assistance is required in a specific situation, the services of a competent professional should be sought to ensure that the situation has been evaluated carefully and appropriately. The author and the publisher disclaim any liability, loss, or risk resulting directly or indirectly, from the use or application of any of the contents of this book.**

FT Press offers excellent discounts on this book when ordered in quantity for bulk purchases or special sales. For more information, please contact U.S. Corporate and Government Sales, 1-800-382-3419, corpsales@pearsontechgroup.com. For sales outside the U.S., please contact International Sales at international@pearson.com.

Company and product names mentioned herein are the trademarks or registered trademarks of their respective owners.

Printed in the United States of America

First Printing April 2011

ISBN-10: 0-13-430241-9
ISBN-13: 978-0-13-430241-6

Pearson Education LTD.
Pearson Education Australia PTY, Limited.
Pearson Education Singapore, Pte. Ltd.
Pearson Education Asia, Ltd.
Pearson Education Canada, Ltd.
Pearson Educación de Mexico, S.A. de C.V.
Pearson Education—Japan
Pearson Education Malaysia, Pte. Ltd.

Library of Congress Cataloging-in-Publication Data is on file.

This product is printed digitally on demand. This book is the paperback version of an original hardcover book.

To my family and friends who have supported me during my entrepreneurial endeavors. Without you, this book wouldn't be possible.

# Contents

# Acknowledgments

First, thanks to my family and friends for supporting me during the road to getting this book published.

Thanks also belong to Tom Reese for his mastery of the English language and his help editing my work.

Another special thanks goes to Kristin Bouton MacLaughlin of KBM Innovations for her great efforts.

I'd also like to thank Jeanne Glasser of FT Press/Pearson for believing in my book and pushing it through to publication.

Special thanks also go out to TickerTech.com for generously providing the stock charts used in this book.

Finally, I'd like to thank our content partners at Dividend.com, namely, TheStreet, Forbes, and NASDAQ, for syndicating our content on their great sites and helping spread my message.

# About the Author

**Paul Rubillo** is the Founder and CEO of Dividend.com, the #1 source for long-term investors. Paul's daily content is featured on such major finance portals as TheStreet.com, RealMoney.com, Forbes.com, AOL Money & Finance, and NASDAQ.com. Paul was also formerly the exclusive author of the NASDAQ.com daily e-newsletter "NASDAQ Stocks to Watch."

Paul is well-known for breaking down key stocks, themes, and trends in an easy-to-digest style, encouraging investors to understand and take advantage of short-term gyrations while focusing on long-term investment goals. Paul motivates readers to take action within their financial lives today so that they can stay ahead of any impending movements in the market tomorrow.

Prior to launching Dividend.com, Paul was a highly successful stock trader who managed his own capital for more than 13 years of full-time market experience.

# Preface

I have always been a passionate entrepreneur. My entrepreneurial spirit was one of the things I inherited from my dad, despite his apprehension about the path I chose in my quest for success.

My father was a 24-year-old immigrant who came to the United States from Italy in 1966 with barely a penny to his name. Within his first three months in America, he met and married my mom and then opened his own successful barber shop in Yonkers, New York, without speaking a word of English. Two years later, I was born.

Yonkers was a town of great diversity and brutal honesty. People were real, never artificial, and weren't shy about sharing their exact opinions about what you were doing. If they thought your work weren't any good, they'd tell you so, using the sort of simple language and sheer candidness that only old school immigrants use. Their harsh words taught me not to be too sensitive, which became a big help to me in the business world, where starting a new venture almost always means facing lots of "no's" along the way.

After graduating in the top 10 percent of my high school class in Yonkers, I decided to put off going to college and instead took my crack at starting a career. I was always interested in making money, and I wanted to get a feel for what opportunities were out there—but first I had to convince my parents I wasn't doing something crazy. You could say they were my first real sale.

Back in the day (the early 1980s for me), I found myself in a "who you know" environment that determined the employment paths of several family members and friends. Being a barber, it seemed like my dad knew everyone, from senators to police commissioners, and my first two employment connections came directly through my father's scissors. I worked for the U.S. Postal Service delivering mail for about nine months until I realized that the *slower* you worked, the more money you made—hardly the way I wanted to spend my life.

Another city job on a trash truck lasted a mere two days. I'll never forget the woman who came out with cold beverages for us at eight o'clock in the morning. When I got in the truck and opened the brown bag, instead of water or Gatorade, she had gladly supplied my crew and me with a six-pack of beer! Then, on my second and final day on the job, I gashed open my arm with an exposed can lid that had been poking out of a garbage bag I'd picked up. This was definitely not going to be my life either! At that moment, I told myself that I was taking charge of my own life. I was more than ready for a different direction.

I was putting the thought of going to college further and further out of my mind, and instead focused on getting myself into a spot where I could own my own business. Becoming a business owner became my primary goal, and I was willing to do whatever it took to make my dream happen. I had a couple of friends that worked in the deli business, and I knew they enjoyed their work and made plenty of money. My parents thought I was crazy for wanting to stand on my feet for 14 hours a day, but I learned the business inside and out, and then a bought my own deli in nearby Dobbs Ferry, New York.

I put everything I had into my new business, working seven days a week for the next five years, taking only six days off during that entire time span. I did very well there, and I loved my work. There were several challenges to tackle each day, including dealing with dozens of vendors and the ever-changing wants and needs of my customers. There truly is nothing quite like owning a business in the state of New York. Back behind the counter, I felt almost like I was on stage each day, entertaining the customers through our lively conversations, which often centered on New York sports teams. The passion that New York sports fans have for their teams make for some of the most colorful conversations you could ever hear, and I thrived off of it. I enjoyed my work and the lasting friendships that came along with it.

Then one day, a financial planner stopped by my store back in the mid-90s and convinced me that I should think about investing my money. My wife and I had just had our first child, and I knew it was time to really start planning my future. I invited the financial planner over to my house one night to discuss things further, and I wound up asking him so many questions that I had his head spinning. By the end of the night, he told me he had a feeling that in a few years I would know more about investing than he did. Was he ever right!

I quickly set my mind to learning everything I could about investing. Within a year, I was enjoying great success as a part-time day trader and felt financially secure enough that I decided to sell my business to one of my employees. I decided to take my capital that I'd worked so hard to earn and become a full-time investor in the stock market. I had been reading every book about investing that I could get my hands on, and I was more curious about things that could go *wrong* in markets, rather than just what a bull market was about. The market was doing really well at the time, and we were about to head into an amazing run fueled by tech stocks, Internet IPOs, and seemingly anything else that had a one, two, three, or four-letter symbol attached to it. I was already making money in the markets, but I had worked extremely hard for my capital, and the last thing I wanted to do was just throw it at any stock and expect it to go up.

Many investors at that time weren't nearly as disciplined as I was, and foolishly held onto stocks for way too long. Novice investors often think things such as "Why should I sell it at $80, when I could have sold it for $110 last week?" The lack of a sell discipline was a major reason many day traders from the late 90s disappeared—they would make money on ten different trades but then give it all back with one gigantic loss.

By 1999, I realized that the stock market was showing signs of the many manias that I'd heard about in the financial books that I'd been reading. At every party or social gathering I went to, people talked to me about the stocks they owned, and it was apparent to me that they didn't know what they were doing. The handwriting was on the wall. The market soon imploded, and many people who previously thought they could trade for a living had to go back to reality.

I, on the other hand, was still playing the market well. People felt they had to commiserate with me for still being in the market, but I was making money. Many investors didn't even realize they could make money when the market went down! I kept my trades simple with just buys and shorts (positions that would make money if the stock fell), and never ventured into the more-complicated world of options. I stuck to what I knew best, and that was gauging the market on a daily basis. I continued trading for the next several years; then at the end of 2007, I reached another significant point in my life. When my daughter was asked what kind of work I did, she said, "My dad doesn't work. He does stuff on the computer."

With that, I was ready for another business venture. I missed being in the public eye. And I wanted to do it online, because I felt that was where everything was already heading. Living on the water had been a lifelong dream of mine, and I had since moved with my family to the town of Smithville, near the Jersey Shore. I got together with a friend who was a web developer, Tom Reese, and spoke to him about going national with my stock research, focusing on rating dividend-paying stocks through our own mathematical paradigm. We wanted to focus on long-term investing with dividend stocks because that has historically been the best possible investment route for the vast majority of the general public. That was when I came up with the idea for Dividend.com, and after several months in development, we launched our new website.

Only one month later, we arranged a meeting with a giant in the financial media space, TheStreet.com. My partner and I traveled up to New York City, and by the end of the meeting, we left with an oral agreement to syndicate our dividend stock content on TheStreet.com. As I walked out of there later that day, I knew we had something special on our hands.

Access to much of the daily content on Dividend.com is free, and we generate revenue from the website by selling advertising space and through a subscription service called *Dividend.com Premium*, where users pay a fee to access our proprietary stock ratings and other members-only content. We've purposely made our website easy for almost anyone to understand and follow. At the end of the day, I feel like I'm helping people secure their financial futures, and I'd like that to be my legacy. My goal from the outset was to build a third-party stock research platform for the masses, and six months after our launch, we were attracting 200,000 monthly visitors. Our stock-picking formulas and other proprietary research tools make it easy for me to judge what a specific investor should do about investing in specific stocks. Nobody's perfect, but my experience tells me that if I tell someone to get out of a stock at $30, the price will probably hit $20 before it sees $40. I don't care if users buy or sell—I'm interested in helping the people who visit Dividend.com, and every day I wake up excited about what I'm doing.

The stock market can be difficult to navigate, but with Dividend.com—and especially this book—my goal is to make investing as un-intimidating as possible. The goal of this book is to share my investing experience with the public to help people secure their financial futures and become what I call a *Dividend Millionaire*. In the following chapters, we cover topics ranging from how to reduce expenses, to my rules of stock investing, and finally, how to grow your money over the long term and retire financially secure. I truly hope this book inspires you and provides insight into what it takes to be a successful investor.

I want to thank my parents, Michael and Anna, wife Danielle, kids Sonia, Olivia, and Michael, partner Tom Reese, and friends that have believed in the dream that I've had and stuck by me the whole way through. Now, let's roll up our sleeves and get down to what you need to know to secure your financial future!

# Introduction

## Lessons Learned and Why You Need This Book

My goal is for this book to be your financial guide in any sort of economy. Whether you are investing in a bull (up) or bear (down) market, the focus should not be about minimizing losses, but rather achieving positive results. Investing is about thriving, not surviving! I have found that investing books tend to run in spurts based on the current investing environment of the latest trend or the flavor of the day. Every market has its ups and downs, and you can ride out the storm and make money even in down times—so long as you are prepared. I hope this book can help you remain grounded and focused in your investing, regardless of outside economic factors.

As an investor, you always need to have two key assets: *discipline* and *respect* for your money. Those are your two biggest allies in becoming a *Dividend Millionaire*. You also need to invest without emotions. If a stock has done well for an investor, sometimes it can lead to a strange allegiance that holds investors back from selling their shares. This sort of emotional attachment is a dangerous enemy of successful investing. Some investors feel like they're dumping their pet at a kennel when they sell a "loyal" stock, but always remember, no matter how well a stock (or any other investment for that matter) has done for you, it is still *not your friend*. Don't ever let your emotions cloud the vision of your main objective of long-term financial security.

A wise man once said that "the only true constant is change." Just as things change in life, investment cycles change as well, and flexibility and discipline are your allies in adapting to change. This doesn't mean you have to get in and out of stock positions on a daily basis, but you do need to be cognizant that things *will* change as time moves on. As we go through natural cycles in the market, what is hot today may not be hot in the next two years, or even the next two months. Regardless of your investing time frame, you must be willing to go with the market flow. To be successful in investing and achieve positive results, you need to remain flexible and have the discipline to say goodbye when things are not working anymore.

# The Tough Realities of Modern Retirement

If you want to retire comfortably, you need to take the lessons contained in this book to heart. Retiring is more difficult than ever, and some startling data has come to light in recent years:

- A recent study by Towers Watson found that the value of total retirement benefits provided to new salaried employees between 1998 and 2008 in the eight industries it surveyed declined by 19%. Increasingly, both public and private sector employers are cutting costs by slashing workers' benefits—making it harder and harder to count on a pension or 401(k) to pay for your retirement.
- Since 1983, Social Security cost-of-living increases have averaged only 3.27% per year. In 2010, Social Security benefits were not increased at all, for the first time in the 35-year history of the cost-of-living program—despite an estimated 6.2 % increase in the everyday expenses of most Americans! Unfortunately for many, the government announced there will be no Social Security benefits increase for 2011, either.

- People's faith in the Social Security system is rapidly dwindling, according to a Gallup Poll in July 2010. Some 60% of nonretired U.S. adults do not believe the Social Security system will ever pay them a single benefit when they do retire. Meanwhile, 56% of current retirees believe their Social Security benefits will be cut.
- As a country, we are getting older. In 2010, around 16% of the population was 62 or older—and most were eligible for Social Security. By 2020, though, 20% of the population will be 62, and that number will swell to 30% in 2030! Where is the money going to come from to pay for the retirement benefits of so many additional seniors?

I'm bringing these statistics to your attention to help you realize just how important it is to take control of your own financial future. Retirement is no longer an issue you can leave in the hands of your employer, or the bank, or the federal government. The handwriting is on the wall – in the years to come, it will be *expected* that people make most, if not all, of their own retirement arrangements. The personal finance and investing lessons I'm going to share with you will give you a head start on this process.

# Why Dividend Investing?

After well over a decade successful full-time trading, I came to a realization that dividend stocks were the best possible investment vehicle for the vast majority of the investing public. That's because dividend stocks

- Pay investors just for owning the stock
- Provide the rare combination of capital gains (price appreciation) and cash flow (dividend payouts)
- Can be used for long-term compounding returns or as an income source
- Are more stable and protective than nondividend stocks because high-quality dividend names have large, dedicated shareholder bases who hang onto shares for a long time

- Provide inflation protection because companies tend to increase dividend payouts when they gain more pricing power
- Work in any economic environment, returning an average of 11% over the past 80 years
- Almost always outpace other yield-focused investments such as bonds, CDs, and savings accounts

As you can see, the reasons for owning dividend stocks are numerous. Plus, it's probably a lot easier than you think to become a *Dividend Millionaire*—all the lessons you need to learn about saving money, putting it to work for you, and growing it over the long term are contained in the pages of this book.

Do you want to be a *Dividend Millionaire?* Everyone does, so let's get started!

# 1 ───────────────────────

# Lessons to Learn from the Recent Economic Downturn

An economic downturn is not always a bad event if we can learn from our mistakes and make the necessary changes. In one way or another, all of us played a role in creating the economic crisis of the late 2000s (and subsequent fallout), but hopefully we've learned a few lessons as a result. Economic mishaps can easily reshape an entire generation's beliefs about the nature of the economy and the risks involved. Just ask anyone who experienced the Great Depression—many of those frugal folks still save rubber bands and tin foil! The unfortunate truth is that we tend to change only our personal spending and saving habits if we personally experience an economic crisis. I have outlined the eight lessons that we all should take away from the most recent economic calamity. These lessons can become essential tools during your journey to becoming a *Dividend Millionaire*.

## Lesson 1: Refrain from Wasteful Consumer Spending

As a result of the housing bubble and easy credit availability, consumer spending increased every year from 1993 to 2009. This spending increase was largely fueled by the run-up in home prices, which enabled home-owning Americans to borrow against the equity of their homes. In quite a number of cases, borrowers were given loans at or even above the value of their homes. For some foolish reason, banks and homeowners alike were expecting real estate prices to continue to rise forever. Consumer credit in the form of credit cards and other loans also expanded significantly over the past decade and a half.

Seemingly everyone was spending like a drunken sailor with no fallback plan. Many were living paycheck-to-paycheck and yet still maxing out their credit cards and lines of credit to purchase items that they wanted but didn't necessarily need. We pinned our hopes on an economic surge that was expected to continue indefinitely. It was like being at a great party, but the party was starting to get out of hand. No one wants to be the first to abandon the euphoria, especially if the party is still going strong.

As noted before, people took money out of their homes because real estate prices were driving higher. In most cases, people didn't invest that money—they took it and bought things that they wanted: a new flat-screen TV, a home theater system, new cars, and for some people, multiple vacations. Suddenly, it was like everyone who owned a home felt like they had a blank checkbook. People were living beyond their means, and no one seemed concerned about real estate prices rising far faster than salaries could keep up with. Life was good, and spending was the norm. But now that the housing market has collapsed, and the credit markets are frozen, many people are living in fear about how they will survive if they lose their jobs—assuming they haven't lost them already!

## Lesson 2: Choose Cash and Carry and Avoid Shop and Burn

During the recent buying mania, many people got into a habit of holiday spending 365 days a year. Now, most are forced to stop and think before they spend. I want you to take that one step further, and stop using credit cards for your purchases. Instead, pay with cash and leave the credit cards at home. Plan your shopping trips out ahead of time by determining exactly what you need to buy, and bring along enough cash to cover your expenditures. Psychological tests have shown that when we pay using plastic, there is an intellectual detachment—the payment doesn't seem real until you get the actual statement. When you pay with cash, however, there is a real connection to the purchase. You literally see your hard-earned money coming out of your wallet and into the cash register of the merchant. When you hand over $180 in cash to a clerk for a couple of shirts at a department store, you get an instant reality check about the true cost of what you're purchasing. Preplanning your shopping trip and using only cash helps minimize impulse buying because you simply don't have the funds available to purchase any items beyond your planned shopping list. When you complete your shopping, your cash is gone, and it's time to go home. When you purchase using credit, on the other hand, it is far too easy to get distracted by your wants rather than your needs.

# Lesson 3: Use a 48-Hour Rule with Impulse Buys

You wouldn't invest in a stock on impulse, would you? Well, you shouldn't shop on impulse, either. A lack of financial discipline across the board is what created our recent financial crisis. To emerge from the economic downturn successfully, I need you to become a smart, disciplined shopper. For any unnecessary purchase over $100, I want you to walk away from the merchant and give yourself 48 hours to think over the purchase. If you still can't live without the item after 48 hours, explore some lesser-priced options that can provide you similar pleasure. During this cooling off period, ask yourself if buying is the only option. Is it possible to borrow it from a friend, a neighbor, or a place such as the library? Would renting it be less expensive in the long run? Do you have something else already on hand that can be used to perform the same task? Buying is only one of many options when it comes to getting things you desire.

I also want you to get into the practice of looking at the long-term cost of an item rather than just the initial purchase price. So for example, rather than buying a brand new car, consider purchasing a used car. You still get the new car experience, the new car smell, drive the type of car you want but you are paying significantly less for the same item with a few extra miles on it. You still get the reward, but you get a much better value. Waiting 48 hours allows you to truly consider a potential purchase and removes the pressure of having to make quick emotional decisions. The next time you walk into a store, I want you to compose yourself and embrace window-shopping as a smart alternative to digging yourself further into debt.

## Lesson 4: Embrace this Four-Letter Word—SAVE

While we were busy living the good life, we forgot all about the way people used to build true wealth in the past: SAVE first; SPEND second. Many of us wound up working only to buy material posses-sions. We forgot the crucial step of saving to build up a big nest egg and then waiting to purchase when we could safely afford it. America as a whole strayed away from a save-first strategy at least partially because of the mythical magic potion that everyone was counting on: the never-ending escalating home value. Banks were urging people from any economic background to tap their credit to buy a new home or tap the equity in their existing home—and consumers did so in droves.

Saving responsibly quickly became a thing of the past as more and more of us plunged further and further into debt. After the bub-ble burst, home values plummeted, jobs were lost, and millions of hard-working people suddenly found themselves in economic peril.

In Chapter 2, "Paul's Ten Step Plan to Financial Stability," we explore a slew of ways for you to maximize your income so that you can save more.

# Lesson 5: Take Responsibility and Do Something About It!

Leading up to the recent financial meltdown, many of us adopted the mindset that the economic euphoria was going to last forever. Despite warning signs all around us, we continued to spend and accumulate debt. We all heard the stories of people with bad credit and low income inexplicably securing huge loans from just about any lending institution to finance the purchase of a new home or a new car—neither of which they could actually afford.

That's not to say hard-working folks don't deserve to have a nice home or a good car—it's just that on paper, most of them didn't deserve the loan that they received. We may have thought it, but no one stepped up to say that maybe there was something seriously wrong with this system. How did banks forget the most basic rule of lending? (Don't make a loan to someone who can't pay it back.) How could people with credit problems suddenly secure a huge loan? What made people think they could afford such a purchase in the long run? Clearly, we were headed for trouble. Still, no one seemed to want to put an end to the madness and take responsibility.

# Lesson 6: Ignore the Joneses—Chances Are, They Don't Own It (The Bank Does)

Life isn't a competition over who has the most stuff. He who dies with the most toys doesn't win anything except the same pine box as the frugal person next to him. That's why it's important to concentrate on your family's needs and not on the possessions that your peers are spending their money on. Just because your neighbors bought the latest expensive item doesn't mean that you need to go out and buy something on par or better. Here are two misconceptions about high-ticket purchases: 1) the buyer can afford it and 2) the buyer actually owns it. You'd be surprised what your neighbor actually owns, versus what the bank that financed the purchase owns. Most of the Joneses this day and age are just digging the hole of debt deeper and deeper. Ignore the competitive purchasing cycle at all costs because "buyer's remorse" is a frequent follow-up to large purchases.

Ask people how they feel about their new car the day they purchased it, and almost without fail, they'll tell you "I love it." Ask the same people how they feel about their car three months later, and they'll usually have a different response like "Oh, it's pretty good." A year into their purchase, the response will be even more muted, and so on. Sentiment about a recent purchase quickly degrades (and so does the item's value!), so before you make a significant buy, ask yourself if you'll still "love it" in six months or a year as much as you do today. If the answer is no, be sure to think twice. Consider delaying the purchase until you *really* need it, or perhaps look at lower cost options such as slightly used items. When you come to terms with how you truly feel about any purchase, you can more easily to determine if the item is a true necessity or just a mere desire that might provide you with a temporary sense of fulfillment.

# Lesson 7: Take Charge of Your Finances; Then Invest

I've heard it over and over again from dozens of investors: "I'm just too afraid to get back into the market; I've lost so much money already." I have only one response to that statement: You're missing out on a tremendous buying opportunity. Three years ago, investors would've been tripping over each other to buy blue-chip stocks at a

50% discount to their historical highs! This is a time in the markets to think about stepping *up*, not stepping *away*. Be honest with yourself: Are you really afraid to put money into the markets, or are you simply not in a good financial position to invest?

If you don't have the money to invest, take the steps now to correct your situation. Don't let fear keep you trapped in a cycle of financial peril, and never plan on a government program to come along and bail you out. If you want to become a Dividend Millionaire, you need to take charge of life and your finances. Do whatever you need to do to get your financial house in order. If you can't afford to live where you do, figure out how to move to a more affordable place. If your car payments are too high, trade in your luxury sedan for a compact that gets great gas mileage. The harsh reality that many are unwilling to face is that sometimes we have to take a step back before we can move forward again. It's a simple equation: If you can barely keep up with your bills, you'll never free up the funds needed to invest. To secure a financial future for you and your family, you need to reduce your expenses and begin to dig your way out of debt first. Don't think about it—take action now.

## Lesson 8: Grab a Shovel and Start Digging Yourself Out

Any financial mess created by overspending can be remedied by simply cutting back. The first step for many people is to stop thinking of "budget" as a dirty word. Budgeting may seem like tedious self-trickery meant for those with mere pennies to their names, but everyone can benefit from setting spending limits and sticking to them. If you figure out your fixed monthly costs first, you'll always have a precise idea of how much you can spend on nonessentials. This is how good businesses operate, and if you work on a budget, you'll turn financial black holes into easy-to-handle small financial pinches that can eventually lead to a clean slate.

To find out what's draining your finances, you need to keep track of where your money goes. I know this may seem like lot of work at first, but I want you to start thinking of your household as a public company and yourself as the CEO. On Wall Street, every company is required to report its earnings (or losses) on a quarterly basis so that the public can assess the job they are doing. Similarly, you should perform a self-assessment on the job you are doing every three months. Just like a business, if you are in the red, you need to sell assets or reduce expenditures. If you were an analyst reviewing your personal quarterly report, how would you grade yourself? Would you recommend your business to others? Each quarter you should present your results to your family members, just as a business delivers its report to shareholders. If you are doing well, you will have money to save, invest, and use toward your household goals. If you're operating at a loss, however, you need to make some hard choices—ideally together as a family.

In the next chapter, you find my plan for Financial Recovery. In a simple seven-step program, you learn how to effectively budget your income, make compromises, and adjustments to your spending habits to ensure you can begin saving and investing toward your future. This exercise reveals any excess spending habits you may have and offers alternatives to help you save money and maximize your profitability. If you follow these steps, you'll be well on your way to becoming a Dividend Millionaire!

# Paul's Ten Step Plan to Financial Stability

## Step 1—Identify the Income Coming into Your Household Corporation

Enter in the following chart all income that your household receives on a monthly basis.

| Income | Monthly Amount |
| --- | --- |
| After Tax Pay | |
| Rental Income | |
| Dividend Income | |
| Interest Income | |
| Social Security | |
| Retirement Income (Pension, IRA, 401K) | |
| | |
| TOTAL | |

# Step 2—Identify Your Necessary Operating Expenses

Enter in the following chart all your necessary expenses. Necessary expenses are food (including water), shelter, and clothing, plus the essentials needed to work so that you can provide those basics for your household. That means that the TV (and virtually every other gadget in your house) is a desire and not a want.

### Necessary Operating Expenses Table

| Necessary Expense | Monthly Amount |
| --- | --- |
| Rent/Mortgage | |
| Property Tax | |
| Home Owners Association/ Maintenance Fee | |
| Utilities (gas, electric, water) | |
| Cell phone/Landline | |
| School Tuition | |
| Medical Insurance/Medical Bills/Co-Pays | |
| Car Payment | |
| Gas | |
| Tolls/Parking | |
| Car Insurance | |
| Public Transportation | |

**Necessary Operating Expenses Table**

| Necessary Expense | Monthly Amount |
|---|---|
| Bank/Personal Loans | |
| Student Loans | |
| 401K Loan | |
| Home Equity/Line of Credit Loan | |
| Credit Cards | |
| Groceries | |
| Clothing for School or Work | |
| Internet/TV | |
| Childcare | |
| Life Insurance | |
| Pet Food/Vet | |
| Misc. Necessities | |
| TOTAL | |

# Step 3—Contribute Monthly Income to Savings

Are you one of the few Americans who dedicates a percentage of your income each month to your savings? If so, enter the amount here. If not, I will show you later on how you can trim some of your expenses so that you can start on the road to make saving a habit. Now enter the amount you contribute every month. If you do not contribute to savings, is it because you don't have the money? Enter your response in the chart.

**Necessary Monthly Savings Table**

| Necessary Savings | Amount Contributing Every Month | If You Don't Contribute, Do You Want to but You Just Don't Have the Money? |
|---|---|---|
| Emergency Savings Account | | |
| Retirement Account Contribution | | |
| IRA Contribution | | |
| College Savings Account | | |
| Self-Employment Tax Payments | | |
| Other | | |
| TOTAL | | |

# Step 4—Identify Your Nonessential Monthly Expenses

Enter your other household expenses; these are expenses that are desires not necessities. To get the most from the money that you have, it's essential to have a basic understanding of the difference between desires and needs. Chances are that a lot of things that you assume are needs are only desires you have disguised as needs to justify purchasing them. For each item after you enter the monthly cost, fill in an action you could take to lower or eliminate this expense and the amount you could save.

## Nonessential Monthly Expenses Table

| Desires and Expenses | Monthly Amount | How Can You Lower/Eliminate This Expense? | Amount Saved |
| --- | --- | --- | --- |
| Gardener | | | |
| Snow Removal | | | |
| Dinning Out/Take Out | | | |
| Coffee | | | |
| Alcoholic Beverages | | | |
| Movies | | | |
| DVD Rentals | | | |
| Concerts | | | |
| Sporting Events | | | |
| Hair Cuts/Color | | | |
| Manicures/Pedicures | | | |
| Club Memberships | | | |
| Computer/Video Games | | | |
| Nonschool or Work Clothes | | | |
| Gifts | | | |
| Vacations | | | |
| Subscriptions (newspapers, magazines, online services) | | | |
| Charitable Contributions | | | |
| College Savings Account | | | |
| Other | | | |
| TOTAL | | | |

## Step 5—Reality Check Time!

After you have taken the time to list your income and expenses, it's time for a reality check on how you stand. Next enter your income, necessary expenses, and household desire expenses. If you find you are operating on a budget deficit, you need to go over your household expenses again to see where you can trim. At the end of this chapter, I have list of my picks for painless trimming.

| | |
|---|---|
| INCOME Minus (–) | |
| NECESSARY EXPENSES Minus (–) | |
| HOUSEHOLD EXPENSES = DIFFERENCE | |

## Step 6—Think Rich Actions, Rather Than Poor Thoughts

Flipping through catalogs and going to the mall can make you feel like you need things that you probably can't afford. Instead of having poor thoughts, take rich actions by doing things that offer a sense of well-being.

During my childhood in the late 1960s, my Sundays weren't spent going to the mall. Heck, we didn't even *have* malls back then, and the stores we had weren't even open on Sundays! Instead, Sundays were family days. We would go to church, and then everyone would hang around together, share a meal, and play board games. I believe we all need to take a step back from the daily grind. When I say "daily grind," I don't just mean Monday through Friday. Today's grind has us going 24/7, and many stores have stepped up their hours over the years to accommodate people's increasingly busy schedules. I think people need to step back and take one day a week (or at least a few hours in one day a week) to better themselves. Make this time not about what you need to buy today, make it about advancing yourself.

What are the actions you can take today to make yourself a better person? When I was 16 or 17 years old (in the pre-Internet days), I would go to the library and read about entrepreneurs—who were successful, what traits they had, and how they got to where they are today. I dedicated one day of the week to increasing my knowledge, and that practice has remained with me to this day. It's important to never stop learning, and you won't learn much at the mall. So, instead of taking shopping trips, try to educate yourself. Next, fill out the Rich Action each member of your family corporation is going to take this week.

**Rich Actions for Family Members**

| Family Member | Rich Action Taken This Week |
| --- | --- |
|  |  |
|  |  |
|  |  |
|  |  |
|  |  |

# Step 7—Trade Your Vice for a Less Expensive Option

Every member of your family corporation should abandon the "I buy it because I deserve it" mantra that has too often defined modern consumer spending. Americans have increasingly developed a sense of entitlement about material possessions, which has led to financial vices. Everyone has a vice, an area of weakness that impedes our progress. For some, it's smoking; for others, it is overpriced lattes, shoe shopping, or eating regularly at restaurants. I want all members of your family corporation to list their biggest vice in the next chart—the one thing you can't go without for an extended period. I won't ask you to completely deprive yourself of things you enjoy (although with unhealthy vices, quitting completely is a good idea), I just want you to cut back a little bit. After cutting back, you'll be surprised how much more you appreciate and enjoy vice purchases.

Cutting back spending on vice purchases is one good way to help maximize the money you can save and invest. Sadly, statistics show most Americans don't have enough in their savings to cover even a month's worth of expenses. To avoid this scenario, focus on increasing your savings, freeing money to invest and allow you to splurge on the expenses that you truly care about. Have all family members in the chart enter their vice and how they are going to cut back on the vice. In the third column, write down an activity that you love to do that doesn't cost you any new money. This is an activity that you are going to do to replace the vice you are cutting back on. So for example, if your vice is going to the movies, maybe your activity is watching a movie at home with family and friends. Thus, you are substituting a lower-cost action for a more expensive one, with the outcome— pleasure from entertainment—being the same.

**Substituting Vices**

| Family Member | My Vice | How to Cut Back on My Vice | Replacement Activity |
| --- | --- | --- | --- |
| | | | |
| | | | |
| | | | |
| | | | |
| | | | |
| | | | |

# Step 8—Determine Spending Goals as a Family

Establish a weekly meeting with your family to discuss the spending plan (don't call it a budget) for the months and years ahead. This plan may involve tough choices, such as forsaking a family vacation this year; but focus instead on the guilt-free trip you can take next year after saving the necessary cash. For example, my kids are of Disney World age, but we've vacationed there twice before—it's not like they're deprived! It's OK to say "No" sometimes, and it's a good lesson for kids to learn you can't always get what you want. Life is good. There's no need for constant instant gratification. Parents, take the bull by the horns and take control of family spending. Don't let your children control the ship because it'll soon be headed into the deep waters of debt. Believe me, kids will learn to accept "No" as an acceptable answer, even if it's difficult to hear at first.

# Step 9—Enlist the Help of a Financial Mentor

Everyone has a relative, friend, or coworker who's had financial success. Reach out to someone close to you, and ask them to become your financial mentor. Seek their help for advice or direction in your financial endeavors. I'm willing to bet there are plenty of people in your life who are responsible and trustworthy enough for this position, and it won't cost you a thing. I urge you to avoid the get-rich-quick financial seminars because most of the time, they're not anywhere near the price of admission—especially when sound financial advice can be had from someone near and dear to you for free.

Write down the contact information for your financial mentor next. Within the next ten days, I want you to contact him or her with any personal finance questions you encounter as you continue along the path to get your finances in order.

| Name of Mentor | Phone of Mentor | Email of Mentor |
| --- | --- | --- |
| | | |

# Step 10—Make Your Quarterly Report

Four times per year, have a family corporate meeting to review your progress. All members of your family should help grade the corporation to see if they're on track meeting their goals. If your family is in the red (spending more than you're bringing in), you need to make some difficult choices. If you're in the black (bringing in more than you spend), your next task will be to decide how best to invest your budgetary surplus. Use the following worksheet to help guide your next move.

Is the family corporation operating in the red (deficit)? YES NO

If the answer is yes, what household expenses can the family reduce or cut next month?

```
┌─────────────────────────────────────────────────────────┐
│                                                         │
│                                                         │
└─────────────────────────────────────────────────────────┘
```

If the family corporation is operating in the black (positive cash flow)? YES NO

If the answer is yes, where are you going to put the positive cash flow to work? Savings, investing, or other family goals?

```
┌─────────────────────────────────────────────────────────┐
│                                                         │
│                                                         │
└─────────────────────────────────────────────────────────┘
```

**Family Members That Agree with the Family Corporation Decision**

**Family Member**                              **Signature**

_____

_____

_____

_____

_____

# Bonus Steps—Paul's Picks for Pain-Free Cost Cutting

Don't look at trimming your expenses as depriving yourself. In most cases, you will find by making some minor adjustments you can increase your savings so that you can begin putting your money toward your long-term goal of becoming a Dividend Millionaire.

## *Insurance Discounts*

Following are my favorite insurance discounts that you may qualify for. In many cases, you can save hundreds of dollars per year just by asking your provider about them. Why don't insurers tell you about these discounts upfront? Because they have no incentive to do so. Almost always, you need to physically call and ask about these special discounts if you want to receive them.

### *1. Home/Renters Insurance Discounts*

### Fire and Burglar Alarm Discount

Installing just smoke detectors and dead-bolt locks will allow your insurance company to give you a discount of 2% to 5%, depending upon the company. Adding a local siren/bell alarm or monitored alarm will earn you another 5% to 20% discount off of your annual premium. If your residence has fire sprinklers, this credit can be as high as 15% with some insurers. Living in a gated community also helps protect your home against theft, so most insurance companies provide a 10% credit for homes in a gated community. Be sure to check with your insurance agent to be sure you receive the correct discounts. Generally, these discounts will be shown as a percentage or a dollar amount credit on your policy under the term of protective devices.

### Weather and Natural Disaster Improvements

Making your home or condo more resistant to weather and natural disasters can save you easily 5% to 20% each year on your premium. Build or remodel your home or condo with a tile or slate roof, add storm shutters or special glass, retrofit your foundation to protect it from earthquakes, or raise your home or condo to protect it from rising floodwater. Check with your insurance agent to find out what discounts you are being given and ask about additional discounts that might be available.

### Higher Deductibles

The price you pay each year for insurance can vary by hundreds of dollars, even by a thousand dollars or more, depending on the deductible you choose and the amount your home is insured for. Although a change in a deductible from $250 to $1,000 might save you $200 per year on a smaller home, the savings can easily be 5 times this much on a larger home. So, forget the "luxury" of having a low deductible "just in case" you have to file a claim.

### Multipolicies or Package Discount

Combining your homeowners, condo owners or renters insurance, and your automobile insurance with the same insurance company can often save you 30% of your overall premium. For example, if you pay $800 for homeowners insurance and $1,500 for auto insurance, instead of an annual payout to two insurance companies of $2,300, you will pay just $1,955 to one insurance company. Discounts vary by state and by company, but rarely is it cheaper to have two separate insurance companies. Contact your insurance agent and ask about combining your policies.

## 2. *Auto Insurance Discounts*

### Higher Deductibles

By requesting higher comprehensive and collision deductibles, you can lower your costs substantially. For example, increasing the deductibles from $250 to $1,000 on a newer Honda Accord could easily save you $300 per year, depending on where you live and other factors. Also, the more expensive the vehicle, the higher the savings. Increasing deductibles from $250 to $1,000 on an expensive vehicle, such as a Mercedes, Lexus, or Porsche can easily save a $1,000 per year.

### Low Mileage Discounts

Be sure your insurance company knows approximately how many miles you drive annually. Did your insurance agent ask you how far you drive to work each day but forget to ask you if this is a 5-day work week? If you work 10 hours per day/4 days a week or work from home a few days per week, this will reduce your auto insurance premium— but you have to be sure your insurance agent knows your work schedule. If you change jobs, change colleges, retire or stop working for another reason, be sure to call your insurance agent and let them know this. The difference in premium between an estimated annual mileage of 12,000 versus a lower estimate of 7,000 can be substantial.

### Good Driver Discounts

Some states give up to a 20% discount for drivers who maintain a driving record with only one minor ticket or only one minor accident (not involving injury to another party) in a three-year time period. Don't take unnecessary risks; speeding through the yellow light, the "quick" stop at the corner stop sign, and driving after ANY use of alcohol or drugs. Saving 20% on a $2,000 annual premium is $400 that you can spend elsewhere.

## Multicar Discount

Do you and your spouse or significant other have separate auto insurance policies? You shouldn't if you want to save a substantial amount of premium. A multicar discount can easily be a 30% annual premium discount. If your significant other is paying $1,200 per year and your paying $1,200 per year, combine the two policies and save $720.00 this year on your auto insurance.

## Safety and Antitheft Discount

Almost all insurance companies provide discounts for airbags and antilock brakes and many for vehicle alarm and tracking devices. Although the airbags and antilock discounts are normally included, meaning the insurance company will know if your vehicle is equipped with airbags and antilock brakes, based on information provided by the manufacturer to insurance companies, this isn't true for antitheft devices. It will be necessary for you to tell your insurance agent if your vehicle has an alarm system, a vehicle tracking system, and so on. Generally, the discounts for safety and antitheft primarily apply to the premium paid annually for the comprehensive coverage; however, these discounts can be as high as 45% of the premium. Review your policy and contact your insurance agent to confirm you are receiving the credits you deserve.

## Defensive Driver Programs

Many insurance companies offer discounts of 5% or 10% for drivers over the age of 55 or for youthful drivers who successful complete a defensive driver program. Contact your insurance agent about these programs to inquire about the discounts available.

## Good Student Discount

Most insurance companies apply a significant discount, as high as 25%, to the insurance premium of full-time high school or college students if a "B" average is maintained. Insurance companies may ask for proof of a 3.0 or better GPA, proof of a top 20% of the class rank-ing, proof of a listing on the Dean's list, and so on. The requirements and discounts vary by state and by insurance company, so contact your insurance agent to learn more about what discount is available.

### Reduce Coverage on Older Cars

You may want to consider dropping collision and/or comprehensive coverage on older cars. Generally, if your car is worth less than $3,000, purchasing coverage to "insure the vehicle" may not be cost-effective. Consider the age and condition of your vehicle. Auto dealers and banks can tell you the worth of cars. Or you can look it up online at the Kelley Blue Book Web site.

### Find Out How Your Insurer Assigns Drivers to Cars

The method in which insurance companies assign drivers to cars can make a huge difference in the premium you pay. This is especially important if one of the vehicles on a policy is an expensive luxury vehicle and one of the drivers in the household is a teenager or simply a 40-year driver with one speeding ticket. This is how it works with some insurance companies: If there are three drivers and two cars in your household, some insurers will assign the driver who's the most expensive to insure (the teenager or the adult with the ticket) to the car that's the most expensive to insure. Many companies enable you to make the choice of assigning drivers to cars. Remember, when it comes to the assignment of drivers, just because a driver isn't "assigned" to a vehicle doesn't mean they won't be covered if an acci-dent occurs. For example, if you have a luxury car and the family minivan on a policy and the teenager is "assigned" to the minivan for insurance rating purposes (because you've told your insurance agent that this is the vehicle the teen will be driving), the teenager will still be covered on the luxury car if she takes it to the corner gas station to fill up for you. All drivers can always drive all vehicles on a policy, it is simply a matter of how they are assigned by the insurance company for purposes of determining the premium rate.

## Discounts for College Degrees and Teachers

Some insurance companies have found that drivers with degrees in engineering are lower risks than other drivers. If you have a bachelor's degree in any number of engineering or science-related fields, you can get a discount on your auto insurance premium. If you're a scientist or an engineer with a good driving record, you can save between 10% and 30% on your premium. Also teachers and professors who are members of state education associations or the National Education Association (NEA) or who hold a teaching credential in specific states are offered discounts as high as 30% by some insurance companies. So, if you have a bachelor's degree or work as an educator, contact your insurance agent to see if a discount can be applied to your auto insurance policy. You might find that switching insurance companies is necessary to get the discount because not all insurance companies offer these discounts. However, the annual premium savings may make changing companies worthwhile.

### 3. *Life Insurance Discounts*

There is a well-known phrase in the financial world: "Buy Term, Invest the Rest." To be sure, *if you have dependents, you absolutely need term life insurance.* Period. Term life insurance ensures that those who depend on you will be able to care for themselves should the unforeseeable happen to you. In contrast, whole life insurance is too laden with fees, so I only recommend term insurance. Use life insurance for what it was intended: to support your dependents if you were to die during your earning years, not as a savings account.

If you already have life insurance, but your health has improved since you originally purchased your policy, ask your agent or insurance company if you qualify for any of the discounts listed next. If your insurance provider will not offer these discounts in your current policy, get a quote from a competitive company, but never terminate your policy until you have confirmation in writing that you have coverage with the new policy.

## Nontobacco User Discounts

If you do not use tobacco in any form (cigarettes, cigar, pipe, smokeless, Nicorette gum, nicotine patch) you will qualify for this discount. If you are a former tobacco user and have now quit using it (duration for how long since quitting varies with the each company), you can still qualify for this discount. This discount can be worth up to 50% to 60%, so it is worth checking to see if you qualify—even if it means changing insurance providers.

## Excellent Health Discount

If you are in excellent health, don't use tobacco, have no family history or death due to cancer or heart disease before age 60, you can qualify for the preferred best class. This discount is usually 15% to 25%.

## Volume Discount

Some companies charge a lower premium if you purchase a higher amount of insurance. For example, there may be a rate break at $250,000, another at $500,000, and another one at $1 million. So, if you are looking to buy $450,000 in coverage, ask the agent to quote $500,000 as well. In some instances, the premium for $500,000 may be about same or lower than for $450,000. This is due to a volume discount at $500,000.

### 4. Questionable Insurance Policies

In the casino, they call these "sucker bets" when the house has all the odds in its favor for winning. Please refrain from purchasing any unnecessary or downright useless insurance. Granted, some insurance coverage is absolutely necessary, including home, health, auto, life, and long-term disability. These are policies that any responsible adult should have. However, many insurance policies are unnecessary, impractical, or downright wasteful. Following is my list of the questionable insurance policies that I just can't stand.

### Accidental Death Insurance

Accidental death covers you if you were to die due to something other than disease or old age. But most policies are limited and don't cover all possibilities, so consider a life insurance policy that covers you in most incidences instead.

### Automobile Collision

Auto collision covers the cost of repairing your vehicle if an accident occurs. Generally if you lease or finance the car, collision coverage is mandatory. But consider increasing your deductible if it is lower than $1,000; you will be shocked at how this can reduce your insurance costs. Pay for small repairs yourself using the savings from your insurance premium.

### Automobile Medical

Most states require a minimal amount of automobile medical coverage, which covers you and your family for injuries or death in an auto accident. In most states, heath insurance is secondary to auto medical, so if you have health coverage, don't buy more than the required minimum because you have the coverage anyway though your health insurance policy.

### Critical Illness Insurance

Please don't take out a life insurance policy that pays if you die from a short list of specific diseases, such as cancer. This is like betting on a specific number on a roulette wheel, rather than on red or black: The chances of hitting it are slim. Instead, fund a term life policy that covers you regardless of how you die.

### Credit Card Insurance

Rather than paying for a policy that pays off your credit card debt should you lose your job, use that money to help dig yourself out of credit card debt.

### Life Insurance for a Child

Why would you insure the lives of your children who will in all likelihood outlive you? You need to have a term policy on you so that your family would have income to cover their needs, should you die and no longer provide for them.

### Mortgage Life Insurance

Don't purchase a homeowners life insurance policy that pays off your mortgage should you die. Instead, purchase a term policy so that your dependents can pay off your mortgage.

### Rental Car Damage Insurance

If you have full auto insurance coverage on at least one vehicle, don't take the rental car optional coverage. Your auto coverage usually extends automatically to a rental car.

# Cutting Utility Costs

Following are my top six ways that you can cut your utility costs and save between $500 and $750 annually. That's more money you could be investing!

1. *Install a smart thermostat*—Why heat or cool your home when you don't need to? With a programmable thermostat, you enter your temperature preferences based on the hour and day of the week, and your home is always at the most cost-effective temperature for your needs.

2. *Buy better bulbs*—Energy-efficient light bulbs are more expensive, but they pay off in the long run. Energy Star-rated bulbs use 75% less energy than traditional incandescent bulbs and last up to ten times longer.

3. *Go low-flow*—f you have pre-1994 shower heads, consider replacing them with ones that are more conserving-friendly; you can find it makes a big difference in water usage.

4. ***Plug a leaky toilet***—A leaky toilet can waste up to 200 gallons of water daily, or 73,000 gallons per year. Most of us don't even know when we have a toilet that leaks. Put a drop of food coloring into the toilet tank; if it shows up in the bowl, you've got a leak.

5. ***Seal the gaps***—Why pay to heat and cool the great outdoors? Simply caulk and weather-strip your doors and windows. Also make sure you close the flue damper when your fireplace is not in use.

6. ***Kill a watt-waster***—When not using your home electronics, make sure you unplug them or use a power strip to turn off multiple devices simultaneously. Your home electronics are draining electricity when they're turned off but still plugged into an outlet.

## Bundle Your Internet/TV/Cable/Phone

Phone, wireless, cable, and satellite TV companies are competing like mad to get your business by bundling services at discount prices. Don't forget any package is negotiable, so don't be afraid to negotiate. If you have been a loyal customer, your provider will normally do whatever they can to keep you. Generally, you can save more than $200 a year by simply bundling your services with the same carrier. In addition to paying just one bill, you have only one company to call if you have a technical or billing issue. Also, don't be shy about shopping your utilities to the competition. Many of the best offers are for new customers, so when you know what the competition will give you, go back to your original provider and ask them to match the deal you were offered; in most cases, they will.

## Coupon/Shopping Websites and Other Discounts

Years ago, it was uncool to use coupons; that is no longer true, and it is now the trendy way to shop. More than 34 million Americans per month visited coupon sites in 2008, and the number of coupon-related Web searches doubled. So it's clear more of us are hunting for deals. If you're not a senior citizen, consider shopping with an older relative because many stores have a senior day where your family member can receive an addition 5% to 10% discount when purchasing items for you. Following are my favorite online coupon sites:

> **Coupons.com**—Geared toward grocery and drug stores.
>
> **CouponCabin.com**—Discounts for popular retailers, usable in-store and online.
>
> **RetailMeNot.com**—Shopping tips for certain stores and a shopper forum to post details on one-day sales and new markdowns. RetailMeNot.com also has a downloadable application that alerts you to promotions and coupons when you are on a retailer's Web site.
>
> **FatWallet.com** and **SlickDeals.net**—Both sites focus on electronics but also feature forums and discounts on other items, too.
>
> **PriceGrabber.com**—Comparison shop for your item across multiple online stores.

### Look into Reducing Your Property Taxes

Many homeowners are over-assessed and should appeal their property taxes with their local municipality. You don't have to pay a service to determine if your have been over-assessed, and with a little bit of leg work, you can get your property taxes reduced on your own. Many local governments limit refunds to just the prior year's tax bill, so don't wait to file an appeal. Following are the steps you need to take:

1. Visit your local assessor's office or Web site. There, you can find the forms you need to appeal. You can also find assessments and descriptions of every property in town.

2. Double-check your property's records for errors that may have artificially inflated the assessment. Did the assessor assume your home had more bathrooms, bedrooms, or improvements than you actually have?

3. Compare your assessment with those of similar properties. Don't hire an expert to do this for you; simply ask your friendly neighborhood realtor to do it for you. Most will gladly provide you with comps in hopes you will come to them when you decide to sell your home. If you can find at least five that carry lower valuations, it will enhance your odds of success.

## Cut Car Expenses

Basic maintenance checks can increase the length of the life of your car and can save you immediate money at the same time.

1. **Check your gas cap**—When gas caps aren't firmly closed, gas vapors can escape, resulting in a loss of 147 million gallons of gasoline each year into the atmosphere. So do a simple check to make sure your gas cap closes securely and is not damaged.

2. **Check your oil**—Have you checked your oil recently? Changing your oil on a regular basis extends the life of your car's engine and helps protect it against engine damage.

3. **Check your tires**—You need to check for low tire pressure and tread wear. Low tire pressure decreases your gas mileage and shortens your tire life. Not having enough tread on your tire increases your chance of losing traction and being involved in an accident, which will generally be more expensive than a new set of tires.

4. **Check your spark plugs**—Don't wait to change your spark plugs when your engine has a hard time starting. By putting off changing your spark plugs, you waste fuel, increase exhaust emissions, and reduce power.

5. ***Check your air filter***—A clogged air filter can reduce gas mileage by 10% and decrease engine power. When a filter becomes clogged, the airflow through it decreases, causing a "rich" mixture of too much gas and not enough air going to the engine.

6. ***Check other lubricants and fluids***—Maintaining fluids at the proper levels can prevent unwanted damage to the car and possibly avoid an accident. Most of us check fluids when we run out of washer fluid and can no longer clean our windows or the warning light on our car has turned on. Improper levels can lead to car systems failing and create driving dangers.

## *Cut Investing Costs*

1. ***Beware of inactivity fees***—If you are just an occasional investor, make sure your service does not change an inactivity fee. For example, if you have not done any trades in a three-month period, E°Trade charges investors $40 for the quarter. So read your statements carefully, especially if you have not been an active trader recently.

2. ***Slash high commission with a discount broker***—Most full-service firms charge $30 or more for an online stock trade. Instead, consider using a discount broker; the average fee is around $10 a stock trade. If you are still hesitant, ask yourself if your full-service broker's research is worth $20 or more a trade. If not, go with a discount broker, and use the difference to buy more stock or put into your savings account.

# 3

## What to Know Before You Invest

## Investors Sometimes Get a Bad Start

Investors find their way to the stock market through many different paths. Some investors may not even know they're actually "investing" in the first place because their money is pooled into the markets through a pension or 401(k) plan. Other times, investors get their initial market exposure through a friend or family member with a new job in the financial services industry. Or sometimes, unfortunately, an investor's first stock is a "penny stock"—one of many thousands of securities that can be bought for next to nothing but comes with the hope of future lottery-like wealth. Trust me, these penny stocks almost never work! All too many of these ultra-cheap stocks labeled as the "Next Microsoft" or "Next Google" wind up to be nothing more than a garbage can to throw your money into. I have a strict rule against buying penny stocks, and you should, too.

Opening an asset management account with a family member or friend who has just gotten into the industry also has its share of potential pitfalls. Many times, your newly minted financial service people are raring to go but unfortunately may be a bit "green" when it comes to knowing everything they should know about investing. There's nothing wrong with supporting people you care about in their new endeavor, but always think twice before putting your hard-earned money in the hands of anyone who doesn't have a decent amount of

investing experience. In many cases like these, the company or broker your friend or relative now works for will simply steer you toward
the readymade product that suits the company best. (And in some
cases, companies give brokers an incentive to push specific products.)
Although these types of things are not what investors want to hear,
that is the sad reality of many asset management firms.

**The Bottom Line** is that if you feel obligated to do business with
an asset management company, regardless of the reason, be sure to
open a small account at first. My hope is that when you finish reading
this book, you'll have enough knowledge and confidence to handle
your investments on your own. When you are investing your own capital, be sure to avoid penny stocks. Nine times out of ten, these near-
worthless securities will just eat a hole in your hard-earned money.

# Use Financial Planners Carefully

Don't get me wrong; there are many talented financial planners
out there today. What investors need to realize, however, is that financial planners are not stock market analysts. There are very few, if any,
financial planners in the world who retain the pulse of what happens
on a daily basis in the stock market. The bulk of a financial planner's
day is not spent watching the markets, but instead servicing current
accounts and looking to open new ones—and rightfully so. Stock brokers, newsletter writers, and stock market Web sites like our own
Dividend.com are the ones who spend each day analyzing the market's ups and downs, and these are the types of people and organiza-
tions who you should turn to for your investment advice. The role of a
financial planner should in most cases be strictly relegated to struc-
turing your finances to achieve your overall goals.

If you are looking for objective financial advice, a fee-only financial planner is probably your best bet. Fee-only financial planners are
compensated solely by fees paid by their clients and not by any incen-
tives from outside companies. (For example, asset managers may

compensate financial planners for each client they refer. I consider this a conflict of interest, and that's why I recommend only fee-only financial planners). Financial planners can be paid in a variety of ways: a flat fee or retainer, an hourly fee, a percentage of assets under management, or a percentage of income from investments. The key here is that the planner does not accept commissions or compensation from any other source, except the client.

All too often, you will a financial planners so keen on getting an account open that they may over-simplify an investing strategy. A common piece of advice planners give their clients is to basically "buy a stock index and let the market do its thing." This is nothing more than an easy way to push investors into the automatic-pilot syndrome, and I have never believed in this type of financial laziness. In this case, the planners may not want you to think about individual stocks because they don't want to worry about spending significant amounts of time doing research for their clients. Again, stock market research isn't their business, contrary to what they may tell you.

**The Bottom Line** is to let the financial planners help you structure your finances, and let the market professionals do what they do best, which is stock market research. I strongly suggest that you utilize specialized research tools such as my own website, Dividend.com, to help identity the best stocks to own in your portfolio.

# Real Estate Is Fine, But Stocks Have Always Been Better for Me

When the real estate market was booming from 2002 to 2005, I admit it was tough to sit on the sidelines. At the time, it seemed incredibly easy to make money simply by flipping homes. I actually bought a second home in South Jersey during that period, hoping that my parents would relocate from New York. That plan proved futile, however, as I quickly learned that old-school Italian parents don't make for the best relocation prospects. I vividly remember buying that property with just 10% down and quickly putting some work into it. The home had ocean views and was probably about 40 yards from touching the beach. The real estate market was red-hot and it was proving difficult to even find available professional renovators that could help me update the home. I wound up being at the mercy of the contractors and paying the price they wanted. Fortunately, I completed the renovations and sold the home before the real estate market began to crater.

You could compare the second-home market to high-growth stocks in that it presents bigger risks and bigger potential rewards than more conservative investing. I probably missed getting top dollar for the second home I bought by about 2–3 months, which in real estate terms is pretty much selling at the top. Even so, when I was showing the home to various real estate brokers, many of them told me that my asking price was $100,000 too cheap. My realtor (who is a good friend of mine) told the brokers to bring the buyers over to look at the place if that was the case, and the price may actually go higher—at that time, bidding wars were not out of the question. The reality was that none of the real estate "experts" produced a buyer, and the eventual buyer of the home came from someone walking into the open house.

The entire process of buying, renovating, and reselling the home produced a profit of nearly $50,000 for about six months of work, but it was too much of a headache for me. Plus, I realized that the distraction was not good for my main source of income: stock investing. One of the things I noticed early on with real estate is that if you're not handy (which I am not), you lose a good chunk of your potential profits. In stock market terms, I would equate this sort of thing to paying a broker $50 to execute a stock trade, when instead you can go online and make the trade yourself for just $10. Execute many of these trades over time, and you'll quickly see how much money you are leaving on the table. In short, there's no sense in relying on a broker for advice that is often no better than what you can get by doing your own research.

Investing in rental properties presents a different kind of hassle, namely, dealing with tenants. I much prefer investing and trading in the stock market because I don't have to deal with those kinds of distractions. Plus, when I want to sell, I can just turn on my computer and press the Sell button—no need to call a realtor and fill out a bunch of complicated forms. After my venture into real estate investing, I've found that I now appreciate the ability to get liquid (sell) quickly much more so than before.

**The Bottom Line** is that although we will see times (cycles) when real estate will outperform stocks as an investment, over the long term, I'll talk my chances with the stock market—especially because you can make money with stock investing whether the market is going up or down.

# Make Sure Your Mental Muscles Are Strong

I can't stress this point enough: Make sure you are in a good state of mind when making investment decisions that will affect the performance of your portfolio. This mantra applies to virtually any major decision you have to make in your life.

If you go into your workday with negative distractions, regardless of what profession you're in, you're probably in for a long day—and in the stock market, it could be a *costly* day. To be a successful investor, you must think clearly, and more important, remain methodical in your day-to-day approach. If you know that you have important things to do during the day that will pull you away from the markets, make sure you avoid taking positions unless you're absolutely sure you won't need to make any adjustments during the trading day.

I remember a stock trader that I would talk to regularly was getting ready to go on his summer vacation with his wife and other friends. The market was entering some rocky weeks, so my advice was to clean out his active portfolio, go away on vacation with a clean slate, and then start fresh when he came back. Unfortunately, he ignored my advice, feeling that he would be "missing out" on some key stocks he'd been watching and wound up having the worst vacation of his life. He constantly had one eye on the beautiful beach he was supposed to be relaxing on, and the other eye checking stock quotes on his BlackBerry. Much to the annoyance of his spouse and friends, who chided him for not relaxing, he always wound being the first one back to the hotel and the first one up in the morning to check the market news. He watched as the markets went through a correction and eventually sold out his positions more than halfway through his vacation.

His inability to take a break from the markets cost my trader friend some well-needed relaxation time, and he also suffered losses that he could have prevented had he sold earlier. Of course, things could have turned out quite differently, and he could indeed have made money while on vacation instead of losing it. However, the point here is that when you are heading into any situation that will pull you away from the markets for an extended period, you should strongly consider not committing to any positions. When investing for the long term, you should have a good idea of names that may need to have stop-loss orders put in to prevent any further damage than you would normally have encountered if you were watching the markets closely.

Another key thing to be aware of is that many investors will get sick from time-to-time, and whether it's a normal flu bug or something that requires medical attention, the last thing you should force yourself to have to do it trade around these situations. It's a recipe for disaster. Treat stock trading like any other job—when you're sick, get the rest you need and get on the road to feeling better. The stock market professional needs to think in the same way.

**The Bottom Line** is that you need to have a healthy outlook, mentally and physically, to accurately gauge and act upon the day-to-day action on Wall Street. If you head into your investing day with any sort of distraction, you're automatically at a huge disadvantage. Don't underestimate the effects that poor health can have on your investing—people who are sick tend to cut positions sooner than they normally would, reflecting the sort of cranky disposition that naturally comes along with an illness.

# "Buy What You Know" and Lose Your Shirt

You may already be familiar with the "buy what you know" mantra that many Wall Street mavens inexplicably rave about. I've never understood why seemingly intelligent analysts would endorse such a strategy. In fact, I argue the exact opposite: "Buy what you know" may be one of the worst pieces of investment advice that anyone could follow. Let's take a look at three examples where buying what you know can cost investors dearly.

One common mistake involving this faulty piece of advice involves employees sinking their investment dollars back into the company they work for. Think about the retirement fortunes that were lost when Enron was exposed as a fraudulent operation. Several thousand employees lost not only their jobs, but their entire retirement savings, as well. Enron workers that were heavily invested in their employer made a critical error in putting their entire trust into an operation they thought they knew. This may be an extreme example, but several industries have been devastated lately, including newspapers, radio, and many specialized retailers. How are those employees feeling nowadays about the value of their portfolios? And let's not forget about some of the large tech players that were huge winners in the late 90s, such as Lucent and Nortel Networks, which saw their stocks rise and fall precipitously. I remember hearing stories of employees in these tech companies who maintained they had no clue as to why the stock prices kept dropping because they were always extremely busy at work. Of course, a portion of those employees made small fortunes if they were able to sell some of their holdings during the run-up, but all too many held onto the stock for their retirement. Little did they know what a costly mistake that would turn out to be.

The next type of "buy what you know" investors buy stock based on certain products they like to purchase. In some cases, this practice can be effective, but only when it concerns super-solid brand names that have been around forever, such as McDonald's (MCD) or Procter & Gamble (PG). Even so, buying these stocks simply because you're familiar with them isn't a sound strategy; you still need to be sure you're getting into the stock at a good price point. Overpaying for a stock, no matter how solid the company may be, is a sure way to limit your potential gains. Many investors can also get caught up in their personal feelings toward a company, which is almost always a big mistake. Keep in mind that your love of a company and its products has absolutely nothing to do with the company's long-term financial prospects. The same holds true for the inverse; don't let your distaste for a certain company necessarily sway you away from investing in it. We'll delve into "investing without emotion" in more detail in a later chapter.

The final style of "buy why you know" investing centers around "fad" companies. This investing strategy is the most dangerous of all. Many, many investors have lost a fortune by buying a hot penny stock tip that trades on the pink sheets, or in companies like Krispy Kreme (KKD), Sirius Satellite (SIRI), or Crocs (CROX). These companies saw their stocks enjoy a meteoric rise, only to snap back to reality when the novelty of their products quickly wore off. In the case of fad companies such as these, there is certainly money to be made through short-term trading. Unfortunately, however, most investors are not skilled enough to determine when the stocks' best days are already behind them and wind up being late to the party.

**The Bottom Line** is that "buying what you know" is simply not a sound investing strategy! In the end, your knowledge and familiarity with a company has no absolutely no bearing on its stock performance. If you're going to become a Dividend Millionaire, you need to keep your preconceived notions about companies out of your investing strategy.

# Treat Investing Like Gardening—Seed, Weed, and Prune

Some close friends of mine are really into gardening. They absolutely love to tend to their garden—planting flowers, vegetables, and virtually anything else that grows. Anyone who's done gardening of their own knows that there's one simple requirement for being successful at it: dedication. You can't just plant some seeds, walk away, and expect everything to come out the way you'd like it to. Weeds tend to pop up where you least expect and require continual removal to keep the garden in top shape. Even your best-performing plants usually need continual pruning. In most cases, the difference between success and failure is the willingness to roll up your sleeves and do some work.

It's helpful to apply that same gardener's mindset when it comes to considering your stock portfolio, or even mutual funds. You must be willing to take the time to personally evaluate the companies or funds that you own. If you leave this task exclusively up to a financial advisor, you will likely be disappointed in your investing performance. Remember, financial advisors are in the business of opening new accounts first and then servicing existing accounts second, contrary to what you may hear from professionals in the field. At the end of the day, it's up to you to dig deep into what you've been planting in your investment garden.

I like to tell investors that stocks usually go down for a reason. Of course, there are times when the overall market trend is down, but then there will be times when stocks or sectors break away from the rest of the pack and begin to plummet on their own. This almost always occurs for a good reason, and as an investor tending to your garden, it is up to you to investigate why your investments aren't growing properly. Pay attention to current news and events surrounding the stock's sector. I recommend visiting financial websites such as Yahoo! Finance, Google Finance, and a site like mine, Dividend.com, all of which will present you with articles that can bring you up to speed about current stock and sector happenings. Simply enter a stock symbol in the search box of these Web sites, and you can likely identify the root causes of what is driving the particular holding down. When you figure out *why* a stock is underperforming, the next step is to start pruning. If a long-term fundamental change in the business has occurred, then you probably want to consider a complete removal from your portfolio. Otherwise, decide just how much of the shares you need to trim, and then patiently wait and see if the price grows back. Either way, you need to develop a concise plan of action to maintain your money "garden."

**The Bottom Line** is that your stock portfolio requires just as much attention as an outdoor garden. When certain investments do not grow well, you need to consider uprooting them and placing your money into different areas instead. Investors and gardeners alike tend to get attached to their favorite plants, but in the end, putting good money after bad is the quickest way to keep the weeds spreading and your portfolio from growing properly.

# 4

## Investing Rules to Live By

## Watch What Wall Street Does More Than What It Says

During each trading day, there's no shortage of opinions and analysis flooding from the keyboards and mouths of market commentators and analysts. On television, radio, and the Internet, investors are constantly bombarded with sometimes starkly conflicting opinions. Before the market even opens each day, stocks are already moving, or are about to react to what a just-released analyst's report has to say about a company's fortunes.

When I first entered the investing world, I assumed that if an analyst put a "buy" rating on a specific stock, the immediate reaction from the market would be a nice move to the up side. As time went on, however, I realized that this wasn't necessarily the case. Back in the late 90s, stocks would move big (mostly upward during the incredible tech and dot-com bull markets). A stock like Qualcomm, for example, would close the trading day at $150 per share. The next morning, an analyst would upgrade the stock, and it would immediately see $10 plus gain in the premarket. Back then, as the bull market was taking hold, analysts were notorious for putting gigantic price targets on stocks. I saw analysts putting $400 price targets on Qualcomm, and the stock would rise all the way up to that level in only a few weeks' time, sometimes gaining as much as $100 in as little as five trading days. Then, the same analyst would come out with *another* upgrade of the exact same stock!

The reason I bring up Qualcomm is because that was the stock that made me realize the "game" was coming to a head. In late 1999, while the markets were racking up big gains, the retail (Mom and Pop) investor started becoming aggressive when it came to stock investing. We witnessed an onslaught of books with overtly bullish titles such as *Dow 36,000* or *How to Become Rich with IPOs* leading the best-sellers list.

I remembered my readings about manias and buying panics, and one of the tell-tale signs of an overly aggressive bull market was that the retail investor's badly timed foray into stock investing would become obvious. It certainly became obvious to *me* at the time that the retail investor had gone berserk—I couldn't go to a family function without spending hours listening to people tell me about the latest tech stock they'd bought that had already doubled or tripled. I remember saying to myself, "Oh boy, is this ever going to end badly."

I have one specific memory of a relative who told me he had bought 300 shares of Qualcomm at $500 a share in late 1999. The stock then proceeded to climb another 100 points in three weeks. I told my relative that he should take at least half of his money off the table, if not all of it, meaning that he should sell his stock and reap the 20% gains he'd made in only a few weeks' time. I knew that the market was getting dangerous, and my advice to him was sound. I was astounded at the reaction I received; he acted as if I were trying to deprive him of future gains! The other reason for his apprehension about selling his shares was the big tax hit he would expect from the short-term capital gains. Many accountants at the time were telling their clients that the short-term gains would be heavy, but what those accountants failed to realize was that we were nearing the end of a great frenzy of easy profits. As you'll read about in the next chapter, I've never believed in letting taxes affect how I invest.

Months later, my relative watched in horror as Qualcomm began to pull back, all the while I reiterated to take some money off the table and not let the entire profit disappear. He still resisted, however, feeling guilty that he could have sold at $600, and that selling at $525 was a bad move. Eventually, the stock dropped all the way back down to under $300, and his short-term $30,000 capital gains profits turned into a $60,000 long-term tax write-off.

**The Bottom Line** here is that investors need to take the advice of market experts and analysts with a grain of salt. Remember, a market expert is usually "talking his book" (hyping stocks that he owns) when he makes an appearance on TV or is quoted in an article, and thus these predictions are often nothing more than wishful thinking. We've seen plenty of top Wall Street firms make some terrible calls; in late 2008, for example, Goldman Sachs put a price target of $200 per barrel on oil, despite that oil prices had clearly topped out in early summer. A couple of months afterward, Goldman finally changed its mind on oil, but much too late for many investors who may have taken positions based upon its recommendation.

In general, you should always watch the actual price movements of stocks more than analyst recommendations or even what common sense may dictate. For example, Internet stocks began to rally in 2003, despite what appeared to be quarter after quarter of bad earnings results. Wall Street is always looking ahead in determining stock prices and often begins to either reward or punish stocks well before the news hits the street. So, if you own a stock that has had a big run up, yet the stock stops moving up on good news, it's usually a big sign that the best news has already been priced in—and that means it's time to start trimming the position.

# Invest Like Spock—Without Emotion

Passion and determination are always prerequisites for success, but just as important is a sense of discipline. Discipline can help keep you objective in your observations and keep you working steadily toward what you're trying accomplish. Looking back to my early days as a stock trader, I wanted to succeed so badly that I sometimes made emotional decisions that I would later regret. I simply wanted to prove to everyone that I could succeed as a full-time stock trader, despite the many doubts that would come my way. After a few early losses, I learned to keep my emotions out of my investing, and for good reason: Studies have shown that people can make irrational decisions based on their emotions. A 2003 study conducted by leading financial market research firm DALBAR found that "Investment return is far more dependent on investment behavior than fund performance." In other words, it was the emotional behavior of the investors that was the biggest determining factor for investing success. So, regardless of whether you're investing for the long or short term, the lesson is the same: Be sure to check your emotions at the door. When things aren't going your way, don't get angry. Instead, take a step back, stay objective, and look for better opportunities in other areas of the market.

## Don't Fight the Tape!

Another one of the biggest lessons I learned early and often in investing was to never be stubborn about my investments. When confronted with a losing position, the best thing you can do is listen to what the market is telling you. Whether you're investing for the long or the short term, the idea that you are right and the market is wrong can cost you a fortune. In order words, don't fight the tape! Here's a story from my trading days that illustrates this point perfectly, and it applies to long-term investing, too.

Back in 2000, when the markets were topping out and the foundation of technology stocks was cracking, I received a call from a long-time friend. He's an extremely intelligent guy and very successful in his career. My friend told me he wanted to make some of that "easy money" he kept reading about. (He was a fan of going to the book store and picking up "get rich" books.) As some may remember, back then popular book themes varied from "Flipping IPOs" to "Options Millionaires" to "Get Rich in the Stock Market." The influx of these types of books was truly the ultimate sign of a market top!

My friend began to think that he would be the next stock market millionaire, and I was his tutor. As luck would have it, he started trading and his first trade made him $500 in only three hours worth of work. He was hooked. I remember telling him to make sure he had solid reasoning for every position he took and some strong conviction, too. Like a worried parent, I sat by and watched as his reasons for his positions become less and less logical. His luck continued, however, as his next six trades over the course of five days netted him an $8,500 profit. He ended his first week of stock trading up $9,000, and my worries for him continued to mount. I spent the weekend telling my friend he did a good job, but that he was also getting a little lucky. I warned him several times about the dangers of letting his guard down. When Monday came, my friend took a position once again in a stock called Broadcom—the same stock that worked for him in his previous four trades the week before. It was like watching a bettor at the horse track, with my friend cheering from the stands for his favorite horse. He took a full position in Broadcom that morning and eventually watched the stock close down a couple of points. "No sweat," he said. "Tomorrow, it'll come back." He was wrong.

I told my friend to put a stop-loss order in (an important tool to protect gains and minimize losses that we cover in a later chapter). I also begged him to stick to a discipline of taking losses. Alas, he ignored my advice, and Broadcom closed down three more points on Tuesday. My friend was sitting on a five thousand dollar loss, but he became even more adamant. "Wednesday's the day," he told me. Wednesday came, and this time the trading gods helped him out a little—an analyst upgraded the stock, but it went up only 60 cents on the day. I told him that this lack of price movement in the face of an upgrade was a bad sign for his "Broadcom thoroughbred." Once again, I advised my friend to take the loss and move on. Unfortunately for him, he was determined to prove me wrong. Broadcom continued to get pummeled for the next two days, and my friend's $4,500 loss turned into a $17,500 loss. After his first two weeks of trading, he was now $8,000 poorer. He fought the tape, and the tape won.

**The Bottom Line** is that many of the world's smartest individuals have had their fortunes ripped out of their hands by the stock market, just as my friend did in his earliest days of trading. So, how do smart people lose money in the stock market? The answer is simple: by naively thinking that they're smarter than the stock tape.

# Cheap Stocks Are Cheap for a Reason

Despite recent choppiness, the current economic environment should not cause you to simply stuff your money under a mattress. Although the stock market is (and always has been) an inherently risky place to try to get rich quickly through trading, it is still the best long-term investment for your money. Annual market returns average 7 percent to 10 percent over the long term. When the market is down, it is usually a good time to build your shopping list—essentially, you're buying stocks at a discount to their "retail" price. However, I want you to always look for *quality* stocks to purchase; the old saying "you get what you pay for" usually holds true in the investing world, too.

When you buy cheap stocks, be aware you also buy more risk. Stocks never lose value when their fundamentals are improving. Stocks get cheap because they hit a bump in the road—whether due to a product cycle or an economic cycle. I don't care if it is a good market or a bad market, I always want investors to think quality first. Look for companies that are consistently performing and getting positive earnings results. I don't want you to buy a stock in which the company is regressing from 20% revenue gains to 10% revenue gains to 40% revenue losses. You should look for stocks that go from 15% revenue gains to 10% revenue gains and then bottom out with gains at high single digits, thus avoiding companies that start to operate in the red. Avoiding losses is a big deal for companies, especially those that pay dividends. Keeping afloat is a key component to maintain and consistently raise dividend payouts, which is one of the many issues we address in Chapter 7, when we discuss the process of becoming a Dividend Millionaire.

## Never Use the Word "Hope" When Describing Your Stock Holdings

When I talk to investors about individual securities, I like to listen to see how they describe the names they currently own. Whenever I hear the word "hope" used, I know they have either paid a much higher price for the stock than it is currently trading at, or they own a stock that is banking on a specific news event for good things to happen. Hopeful statements from investors are usually framed like "I hope this stock can turn it around," or "I hope this drug they are working on gets approval for the next phase of testing." Far too many fortunes are lost waiting for "hope" to come to fruition. Keep this in mind when you look at the strength of the names you own; if you base the prospects of your investments on hope, you may need to reconsider your strategy.

If the overall market is down, and investors say things such as "I hope this market can bottom soon," I get a sense that there may be too much money at risk in the market than the investor is prepared to lose. In many cases, hope can turn into despair for those whose portfolios are not prepared for the approaching storms gathering strength to batter their investments. Market watchers and industry professional like to tell investors that things always come back and that you need to "relax and wait it out." The main reason advisors like to use those terms is that they failed to alert you about the storm that was heading your way in the first place!

**The Bottom Line** is that instead of placing your bets and hoping that things go your way, make sure your portfolio is in a position of strength to weather any storms. Nobody's perfect, and in investing, you have to expect to take some hits, but it is up to you to prepare for incoming storms and limit the damage they can do to your portfolio.

# Drawing Lines in the Sand Can Be Disastrous

Stubbornness and an inability to cut losses are the two worst enemies of stock investors. It is the investors' task to fight human nature and keep their discipline, despite the natural urge to "double down" in the face of adversity. When I first moved to South Jersey, I often witnessed human behavior at its finest upon accompanying my visiting relatives to the nearby casinos in Atlantic City.

Having a friend in the casino business, I used to bug him about giving me the inside track to what games held the best odds for me. Besides giving me the usual response (there aren't any good odds), he did give me one strategy that he liked to play on occasion. My friend had a strategy for roulette, where he would bet the "two out of three" columns at the front of the table; he felt those columns gave him the best odds. He also mentioned to watch out for the tables where the green zero was popping up on the digital number tracker, which would kill the strategy. Following his advice, I started watching the digital boards above the roulette tables to see which numbers had come out and move around from table to table if I had to. I tried his strategy out, and I held my own and came out with a few dollars. I knew full well, however, that any betting strategy was inherently flawed because the house would always win in the long run. That's why I've only made my big gambles in the stock market, where I feel more like the "house" than the likely loser.

During one of my infrequent trips to the casino, I witnessed a scenario play out that I would never forget. I was walking around the roulette area and came upon a table where the last nine numbers on the digital board were all red. That means that a red number had been selected nine times in a row, which I'd never seen before. I was wondering if they'd removed the black numbers for a second! I walked over to the table and noticed a group of guys in their early twenties. One of the guys reached for his wallet and cashed in $1,000 on the table for some large chips. My first thought was this guy was going to continue to ride the red wave. Instead, he attempted to buck the trend, and put $200 down on black. The dealer spun the ball, and once again it landed on red. The young man grabbed another $300 in chips, placed them on black, and *again* a red number came up. He started laughing, but was also shaking at the same time. This time, he put $500 down on black, figuring he'd break even on the next spin. The ball spun, and wouldn't you know...it landed on red again. His friends flung their arms up in the air, and the young man stood there stunned. Clearly "drawing a line in the sand," he decided he was going to show his friends and the roulette table who was boss. He pulled another $1,000 out of his pocket, putting it all on black. The ball traversed the table one final time, landing on a green zero, a 37-to-1 long shot. Game over. With that final blow, the young man and his friends finally walked away, their night clearly ruined. I stuck around to watch and see if the black would finally come out after that, but it took two more spins to finally see black.

**The Bottom Line** is that investors often make a similar mistake to that of the young man at the roulette table. When investors think they *know* a certain stock is going to bounce, but then it doesn't, human nature encourages us to draw a line in the sand. This sort of behavior is sure to cost you big-time in investing. Don't ever take a stand to prove a point with the investing gods! I hate comparing the casinos and the stock market, but human nature applies to both places—to be successful, check your ego at the door and learn to cut your losses.

# How to Find Winners and Avoid Losers

## Finding Winners Is Easy, Making Money Consistently Is Hard

The first two questions many people ask when it comes to the stock market are "What should I buy?" or "What are the hot stocks right now?" These questions are more than legitimate; the most important part of stock investing is picking the right stocks to buy. I usually begin my stock search by looking at the "new highs" list (52-week highs) to find out what areas of the market are working well. The beauty about buying names hitting new highs is that there's little overhead resistance, which basically means that there are fewer sellers found in those stocks than in names that have been under-performing.

Contrary to what many investors may think, under-performing stocks are often difficult to make money with. Common sense would seem to dictate that stocks with worse recent performance (and therefore lower prices) would perform better than stocks that have been running up lately. Using that logic, you'd think that the best investing strategy would be to buy stocks as their prices are coming down. This strategy is inherently flawed, however. Let's say you bought Cisco Systems (CSC) when it was breaking down from its all-time highs back in September of 2000. Many investors that never adopted a sell strategy would have bought Cisco at $60, and then more at $50, because it was getting cheaper, and it used to be $80. Cisco stock kept dropping, however—all the way down to $8 per share. At that point, there were mountains of buyers that had been catching the same "falling knife" together. Then, as the stock began to bounce, it was met with loads of sellers who were just trying to get some of their money back. Take a look at Figure 5.1, the Cisco chart since then, and you can see the stock (now ten years later) never passing the $33 levels and closed out the 2008 year at the $17 level.

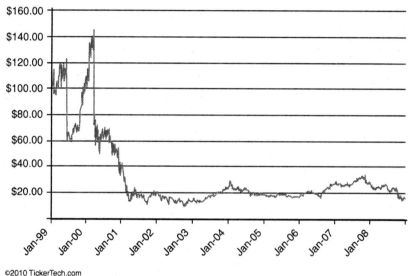

©2010 TickerTech.com

**Figure 5.1    Cisco Systems (CSCO) 1999—2008**

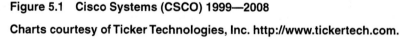

**Charts courtesy of Ticker Technologies, Inc. http://www.tickertech.com.**

Now that I've illustrated why recently under-performing stocks aren't a good place to start looking for investments, I need to mention an important exception to this rule. The only under-performing stocks I recommend looking at are those with high (but not *too* high) dividend yields. We'll delve into dividend stocks in much greater detail in Chapter 7, but in general, I like to scan stocks with dividend yields that are below 8% to see if there are any well-known stocks that may be trading down for reasons that are short-term in nature, meaning that the stock will likely bounce back from its recent underperformance. Let's take a look at what happened to a couple of those blue-chip dividend stocks: McDonald's (MCD) and Altria Group (MO).

Back in 1999, McDonald's was trading at $43 per share (see Figure 5.2). Four years later, the stock was at $14 as the company's stores were floundering. At the time, despite that McDonald's was one of the largest, most recognizable brands in the world, its stock was trading horribly. The company brought in new management in 2004, led by CEO Jim Skinner, and the stock started to perform beautifully again, going up more than four-fold in five years, all the while still paying and increasing its dividend.

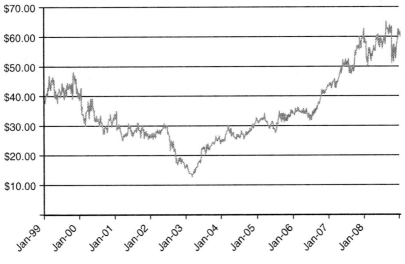

©2010 TickerTech.com

**Figure 5.2   McDonald's Corporation (MCD)**

**Charts courtesy of Ticker Technologies, Inc. http://www.tickertech.com.**

Altria Group (MO), formerly known as Phillip Morris, is another formerly under-performing dividend stock that turned things back around. Back in 1998, Altria Group (then known as Philip Morris) was starting to feel the heat of multibillion-dollar class action tobacco lawsuits, and some investors started to worry that the tobacco industry would be forced into potential bankruptcy from the weight of the litigation. Shares of Altria fell from $55 a share in 1998 to $26 a share in 2000, but the company never stopped paying its substantial dividend, (The stock's dividend yield hovered around the 7% level for much of this time.) Eventually, the lawsuits were settled, and the stock skyrocketed from under $26 to nearly $90 a share within 7 years. Plus, investors who owned the stock during that period saw their quarterly dividend payouts rise more than 50%, as shown in Figure 5.3.

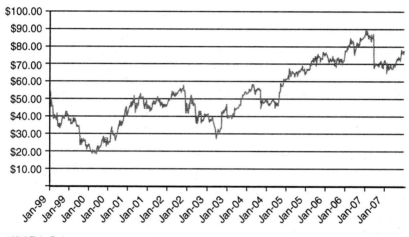

©2010 TickerTech.com

**Figure 5.3   Altria Group (MO) 1999–2008**

**Charts courtesy of Ticker Technologies, Inc. http://www.tickertech.com.**

As the big downturns and subsequent rebounds of McDonald's and Altria demonstrate, there are always investing opportunities in quality stocks whose prices have taken recent, but temporary, hits. The trick to finding the next great buying opportunity is putting in the research time to find these sorts of high-quality names. In following sections, I hope to continue to steer you in the right direction on your journey to pick the right stocks that can enable you to become a Dividend Millionaire.

# Companies with Cash Aren't Always a Good Investment

Many analysts recommend looking for investment ideas by scanning for companies that have a great deal of cash on their balance sheets. This strategy, however, can often lead investors to invest in companies that have no strength in their fundamental business. Back during the dot-com/tech bubble, for example, I saw many reports recommending stocks that were trading at cash-to-market-cap ratios of 25% to 30%. This ratio essentially means that a company's cash in the bank represents 25% to 30% of the company's entire value. Many of those same stocks eventually traded to 70% to 90% of cash because their stock prices continued to drop. More often than not, eroding share prices are to blame for high cash-to-market-cap ratios, and downturns in share price are usually due to eroding company fundamentals.

The most important thing to look at when assessing a particular stock is the future prospects of the company's business. Is the stock living on borrowed time, heading down a path to oblivion, or has the company's stock been mispriced as a result of an overall market meltdown? This is the primary question investors should focus on when trying to find "bargain" stocks.

Some of the big tech names today such as Apple (AAPL), Microsoft (MSFT), and Cisco (CSCO) all have the kinds of big cash balances that make fund managers and investors salivate. When it comes to technology companies, though, cash is good, but innovation is better. Apple has been innovating like crazy in the past several years and has grown its brand to all-time high levels. (Although it still doesn't pay a dividend.) The company had about $27 per share in cash as of January 2009, with shares that were priced around $90 per share. Aside from some concerns about Apple CEO Steve Jobs' health, there is no reason to believe the company won't continue to innovate and stay profitable for many years to come. During the same time period, Microsoft had about $2.50

a share in cash, and the stock was near $20 a share. Microsoft still generates boatloads of cash, but the company has not innovated well the last several years, and that will eventually catch up to any company. Microsoft will likely need to continue spending some of its cash on acquisitions that may help kick its revenue streams up several notches. During January 2009, Cisco had about $3 and change in cash per share, with stock trading near $17 a share. Similar to Microsoft, Cisco has had to use its cash hoard on acquisitions to continue to maintain its networking technology lead. Many analysts fear that Cisco may eventually fall victim to new networking technologies developed by other companies, which could potentially turn Cisco into the next Lucent or Nortel—both once-revered tech names that have long since fallen from grace.

With most technology companies in particular, cash can be a double-edged sword. If complacency within a tech company kicks in, innovation eventually takes a back seat. Take a look at many of the big brands from yesteryear that are now just a shadow of their former selves. Companies such as Xerox (XRX) and Corning (GLW) have struggled in the past few years due to their failure to adapt to changing market conditions and lack of innovation in their domains. Two more examples are Polaroid and Iomega, which dominated in their respective fields at one time but later crashed and burned due to their failure to continue to innovate. Then, of course, there's the one-mighty AOL, which ruled the dialup Internet landscape of the late 90s but failed at many levels to adapt into a viable business when high-speed Internet became the norm. AOL had tons of cash but clearly forgot that innovation was the key.

**The Bottom Line** is that investors should assess each stock on the merits of what its fundamental outlook is and not just on how big its bank account is. Particularly in the technology sector, whenever companies become complacent, they quickly lose their competitive advantage and are susceptible to being passed by.

# Find the Gauge and You Will Find Profits

One of the things I like to do in my daily email to our Dividend.com Premium subscribers is to point out what parts of the market deserve attention, and more important, which of the companies within those sectors investors should have on their radar screens.

Because the market tends to go through rotations, it is essential for investors to be in touch with what sectors are working and what aren't. Sectors tend to stay in their respective trends for weeks, months, and sometimes even years. Investors should concentrate on gauging the importance of these hot sectors in relation to the overall market averages. Let's take a look at some examples. In early 2008, many commodity-related names were consistently popping up in the "New 52-Week Highs" list. Steel, copper, coal, integrated oil, and oil drillers were all flying high at the time. My strategy is to look at the individual sectors and find the stocks that would usually lead the rallies within those sectors, and make those stocks my particular gauges for the entire sector. For the integrated oil stocks, I used Exxon Mobil (XOM) as the gauge. For the oil drillers, I used Transocean Offshore (RIG). For copper, steel, and coal, I used Freeport McMoran (FCX), U.S. Steel (X), and Peabody Energy (BTU), respectively. I found that I could get an accurate gauge of these sectors by closely watching the daily performance of these sector leaders.

Finding a sector gauge is one of the most important things investors can do because it can also give you an early indication as to when a sector may be nearing its top. Short-sellers (traders looking for stocks that will fall quickly) can find big profits by looking at other (nongauge) names in the sector when the sector begins to show signs of weakness. For example, by July 2008, I began to see many of the commodity sectors mentioned in the previous paragraph begin to break down. From a short-selling standpoint, an investor could begin to look at some of the other names in those sectors that are not as strong as our sector gauge for potential shorting opportunities.

**You don't ever want to employ this strategy if the sector is in an uptrend because some of these smaller/weaker companies can get taken over in an acquisition, which would drive the stock price up significantly in a short amount of time.** An acquisition deal is the worst thing that can happen to a stock you're shorting. If you take a look at many of the stocks in the sectors previously mentioned, you can see that many of the names fell anywhere from 50% to 80% from their highs during the commodity boom. This translated into some of the best shorting opportunities we have seen since the Tech and Dot-Com bust that occurred in 2000–2001. Check out the following charts of some of these names, as shown in Figure 5.4.

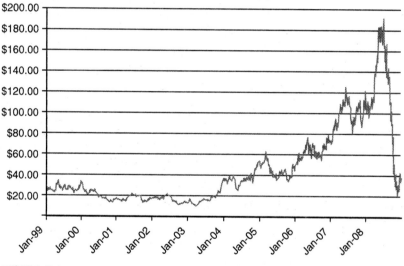

©2010 TickerTech.com

**Figure 5.4   U.S. Steel (X) 1999–2008**

**Charts courtesy of Ticker Technologies, Inc. http://www.tickertech.com.**

One thing to remember when it comes to the "gauge" strategy is that the gauges will always change over time. The stock leading the tech sector today may not even exist in a few years. There are several reasons for this ongoing change, and many times it's simply due to certain companies evolving better than others. For example, if you had told Dell, Inc., (DELL) investors in 2001 that they would see

Apple, Inc., (AAPL) become the hottest consumer play in the tech business by 2007, they probably would have thought that you were out of your mind. In short, the market stays the same, but the gauges end up changing over time. Sectors are in a constant state of rotation, in which we see new companies and industries come to the forefront. Stocks and sectors that are hot today will eventually be replaced by different companies that can uncover better ways of doing business, and then these new names will become the objects of investors' desires.

**The Bottom Line** is that finding a gauge within each major sector will usually lead you to the highest-quality stocks. These names tend to run up higher and faster, leading any rallies within the sector. Be wary of banking entirely on one sector though—what's hot today could be cold tomorrow. On Wall Street, we often see a **sector rotation** take place in which investors move their money en masse from one area of the market to another.

# Ignore the Trend at Your Own Risk

As discussed in the previous chapter, the markets tend to go through different cycles in which certain industries become dominant investment themes for varying periods of time. Wall Street has increasingly become a copycat world, where fund managers and individual investors flock together toward certain sectors. As an investor, it is your duty to identify what areas of the market you need exposure in. A famous saying about the stock market is that "there always tends to a bull market *somewhere*." Even during periods of market decline, there have always been sectors and individual stocks that perform extremely well. A good example of this point is the steel sector's meteoric rise from 2003–2008. Let's look at how well some steel names did.

- **AK Steel (AKS)**—Ran up 3,500% in a 5-year period before the summer 2008 correction kicked in
- **Schnitzer Steel (SCHN)**—Skyrocketed 800% in 5 years
- **Nucor (NUE)**—Ran up 750% in 5 years

- **Reliance Steel (RS)**—Up 700% in 5 years
- **U.S. Steel (X)**—Ran up 1,200% in 5 years

As you can see, the returns in the steel sector during this period were remarkable. Even for investors who didn't sell at the absolute top, and got out of their positions when we recommended on Dividend.com (in late August 2008, about 5%–10% off the top), these were spectacular returns—and all these companies paid dividends. We saw the same sort of runs in the tech sector in the late 90s and more recently with many commodity sector plays. The exciting part of the market is that there is usually *something* out there that will stand out and outperform the rest of the market. The biggest thrill in investing is finding that outperforming sector and acting to profit tremendously from it—that's another piece of the formula to becoming a Dividend Millionaire.

# The Catalysts That Drive Stocks Higher or Lower

Another topic that investors, especially people new to the market, like to ask me about is what exactly pushes stock prices up or down. There are many catalysts that drive stocks higher, but positive earnings growth is usually the primary catalyst to generate interest in companies that can deliver consistent performance. You tend to see some aggressive upside action in up-and-coming growth areas in which earnings may still be small, but the rate of growth from quarter to quarter gets market analysts excited. Analyst excitement, in turn, leads to higher stock target prices—another factor that can encourage a stock to run higher.

There are also times when a new product can send a stock's price skyrocketing, but investors should always be careful when it comes to this type of catalyst. Back in the late 1990s, Viagra became a huge drug for Pfizer, and the result was tremendous press coverage, followed by a few years of outperformance. On the flipside, we have also seen brands shoot up quickly and then fall back down to earth just as quickly. This applies to companies such as Krispy Kreme (KKD), whose doughnut chain grew too far, too fast and Crocs Inc. (CROX), whose mold-injection foam shoes caught on for a quick fad.

Other times, a change in management can make a huge difference in stock price. We saw a big upside move in Hewlett-Packard's stock when Carly Fiorina was replaced with current CEO Mark Hurd in the spring of 2005. Hurd was able to right the ship for Hewlett and made the stock one of the better tech performers in its space. We already mentioned the remarkable turnaround McDonald's made from 2003–2008, as well. The opposite effect can sometimes happen, though, when a well-known CEO retires. Many General Electric (GE) investors long for the days that famous no-nonsense executive Jack Welch ran the company. If you take a look at the company's performance since he retired in 2001 as CEO, the stock has never recovered from losing him.

The other catalyst that can sometimes gear stocks for outperformance is the level of mergers and acquisitions activity that happens in a particular sector. Investors are often drawn to competitors of a stock that has just been announced as a takeover. Market prognosticators get excited when they begin to think about what company in the sector may be the next juicy acquisition target.

A good investor is always on the lookout for good and bad catalysts. There is usually an array of reasons why stocks tend to move up, and many of these same reasons are to blame when stocks begin to underperform, as well. Companies begin to miss on earnings, sectors decline, and talented members of management teams leave for other opportunities. Sometimes you can get an early indication of trouble ahead when senior members decide to leave a company to "pursue other interests"—this can often be a red flag that things are not what they used to be within the company. One of the biggest events that scares Wall Street is when a CFO (Chief Financial Officer) leaves a company. When that happens, there is always concern that there may be some questionable accounting issues afoot, and that the CFO has either done something wrong or refused to alter some of the numbers that other parts of management wanted to tweak.

# Don't Over-Diversify in the Same Sector

We hear the word "diversification" a lot in the financial services industry. Diversification is, in general, a time-tested and sound investing strategy. However, many investors make the mistake of over-diversification within a single sector. Simply put, you will almost never need to own more than two names from any specific industry. The simplest investing strategy within a sector is to buy the two best-performing names in it. There's really no reason to own any more than that. Another common investing mistake is buying names within a sector strictly based on stock price. This is probably the worst way to approach a sector because the cheapest stocks within a sector are almost never the best ones to own. On most occasions, the much more expensive stock will outperform the cheap one. I would usually rather own 25 shares of a $200 stock than 1,000 shares of a $5 stock.

Speaking of price, I like to be blunt when it comes to describing "cheap" stocks. Stocks are usually "cheap" for a reason, and most have earned those low prices with poor company performance. Buying cheap stocks isn't being shrewd; it's being foolish!

Take a look at the performance of Warren Buffet's Berkshire Hathaway Class A (BRK-A) shares in Figures 5.5 and 5.6. You could have bought one share at nearly $6,000 a share in the early 1990s. That's right, $6,000 for *one share*. Sounds expensive, right? Well, those shares hit a high of *$140,000 per share* in 2008 and have since pulled back a bit. Same deal with a tech giant, Google (GOOG), although on a smaller scale. Google debuted at nearly $90 a share in 2004, which seemed expensive at the time. By 2007, however, Google stock was worth more than $700 per share, although it's pulled back significantly from those highs.

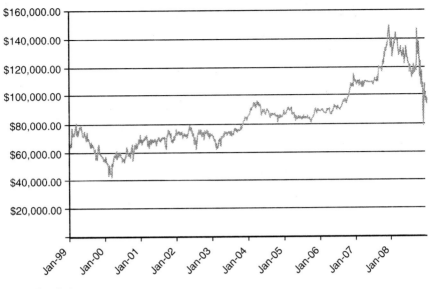

©2010 TickerTech.com

**Figure 5.5   Berkshire Hathaway Inc. (BRK-A) 1990–2008**

**Charts courtesy of Ticker Technologies, Inc. http://www.tickertech.com.**

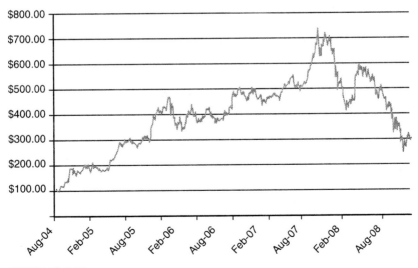

©2010 TickerTech.com

**Figure 5.6   Google Inc. (GOOG) 2004–2008**

**Charts courtesy of Ticker Technologies, Inc. http://www.tickertech.com.**

In summary, investors should buy the best stocks within the sectors that are currently working, regardless of their share price. Just remember, two stocks within each sector is more than sufficient for your portfolio.

# Insider Buying Can Be a False Tell

Following insider buying has always intrigued investors as a potentially good strategy. The people on the inside of a company, however, can often be in denial about the true negative state of their companies. When you look at the sheer amount of equity that disappeared in 2008, you've got to wonder just what the insiders that were buying big blocks of shares were thinking. The phenomenon of faulty insider buying illustrates that there are no sure methods of investing success, and each stock must be analyzed thoroughly, independently, and objectively. Take a look at the actions of some company execs in 2008, which we detailed on Dividend.com.

> This post was written on September 19, 2008:
>
> > One of the biggest bets that has been made is coming from Chesapeake Energy's (CHK) CEO, Aubrey McClendon. McClendon's insider buying this year makes Michael Dell's recent $100 million purchase of Dell stock look like a minor bet, to say the least. Take a look at the amount of buying McClendon has been doing from the end of February, and you will see what we mean by our "all in" headline. Before we get accused of targeting these stock purchases as bad moves, Mr. Mclendon did start buying large blocks of stock in his company when nobody was a believer in it. At that time, the stock [was in the] mid-teens and soon skyrocke[t]ed to a 2008 high of nearly $70 in early July. Check out his insider buying activity this year:
> >
> > - July 15: 750,000 shares at a cost of $57.25
> > - June 11: 200,000 shares cost range of $59.99–$60.08
> > - May 23: 203,000 shares cost range of $54.70–$55.05
> > - May 23: 446,00 shares cost range of $52.45–53.05

- Apr. 2: 500,000 shares at a cost of $45.75
- Mar. 6: 53,800 shares cost range of $45.77–$45.91
- Mar. 6: 46,200 shares cost range of $45.54–$45.76
- Mar. 5: 306,000 shares cost range of $46.13–$46.41
- Feb. 29: 100,000 shares cost range of $45.24–$45.40
- Feb. 28: 100,000 shares cost range of $46.06–$46.21
- Feb. 27: 148,700 shares cost range of $45.61–$46.07
- Feb. 27: 51,230 shares cost range of $45.68–$46.16
- Feb. 26: 7,600 shares cost range of $46.47–$46.55
- Feb. 26: 192,400 shares cost range of $45.65–$46.55

Talk about believing in your company! If he were a trader at a big firm, this style of trading would put McClendon in danger of losing big dollars. Now he did do a lot of buying on the way up, so it's quite possible that he may be still be ahead of the game, but the dangers of fighting a trend is evident in what has happened with energy prices, especially natural gas. This will either be a dollar cost-averaging successful "line in the sand" story, or the very essence of putting good money after bad. Investors may want to watch this game of high-stakes insider buying from the sidelines.

Now look at the follow-up post I wrote on October 11, 2008, regarding Chesapeake Energy, whose shares had fallen to around $16.50 at the time:

> Chesapeake Energy (CHK) CEO Aubrey K. McClendon has sold "substantially all" of his stock in the company over the past three days in order to meet margin loan calls, the company said late Friday. We wrote about his relentless buying of shares back in early September, and we felt this was going to be a huge gamble, especially as he was buying heavily as the stock was drifting lower. Some reports suggested his share total got to 33 million. With the price of natural gas lagging and the energy sector in turmoil, it was a tremendous risk for Mr. McClendon to fight the trend. The lesson for investors is to remember to avoid "fighting the tape," and putting too much in one position. It happens to the smartest of traders and

money managers, as well as even CEOs, like in this case. We will be watching to see how the stock trades now that this news is essentially out of the way.

In the final example, take a look at insider buying at one of the most well-known companies here in the United State (and the entire world): General Electric (GE). This post was written on November 17, 2008:

> General Electric (GE) CEO Jeffrey Immelt has continued his unabated inside buying of GE stock, with his latest purchase coming just last week. The CEO of General Electric has been quietly drawing lines in the sand with his purchases of GE stock over the last two years. Here's a quick rundown:
>
> - 50,000 shares purchased at $16.41–$16.45 per share—Nov. 13, 2008
> - 115,000 shares purchased at $30.59–$30.66 per share—May 28, 2008
> - 62,000 shares purchased at $32.74–$33 per share—Mar. 11, 2008
> - 90,000 shares purchased at $33.40–$33.44 per share—Feb. 29, 2008
> - 35,000 shares purchased at $36.55–$36.62 per share—Dec. 18, 2007
> - 83,000 shares purchased at $40.03–$40.13 per share—Oct. 22, 2007
> - 25,000 shares purchased at $38.80–$39.06 per share—Jul. 30, 2007
> - 20,000 shares purchased at $35.54–$35.54 per share—Apr. 16, 2007
> - 20,000 shares purchased at $36.37–$36.37 per share—Jan. 26, 2007

We have been bearish on General Electric, which has been a name that has lagged on most days. Even in the early summer, when the overall market was at much higher levels, GE stock consistently failed to perform well on the biggest rally days. Such underperformance was a red flag for us.

CEO Jeffrey Immelt's recent insider buying, as admirable as it may be, reminds us of the Chesapeake Energy (CHK) CEO buys that previously caught our eye. It's certainly possible that GE can start righting its ship, but to continually buy shares on the way down is not something most traders should emulate. We'll keep investors posted of any further news that may get us to turn bullish on the name.

General Electric fell all the way to $12 per share by January 2009 but has since recovered from those lows.

As the preceding examples clearly illustrate, investors need to dig deep into the reasons why insiders are buying their own stock. Many times, top executives fail to accurately gauge the severity of their companies' challenges. There have been numerous companies in the recent past whose executives were pummeled as a result of insider buying, including Wachovia (WB), General Growth Properties (GGP), Borders Group (BGP), and many others. And as you learn in the next chapter, knowing when to *sell* a stock is often more important than knowing when to buy.

# 6

## Selling Is a Virtue

## Learn to Sell or Risk Losing Everything

When you ask stock investors if they have the discipline it takes to make money on a consistent basis, without fail you'll be greeted with a quick "Yes." When faced with losing positions, however, we often see evidence to the contrary.

Remember the case of my relative that watched his Qualcomm profits disappear because of his stubbornness of not wanting to sell? He couldn't bring himself to push the Sell button because he felt guilty that he could have sold at $600 and selling at $525 was a bad move. Eventually the stock dropped all the way back down and the short-term $30,000 capital gains profits turned into a $60,000 long-term write-off. Every day, many investors face similar situations. The refusal to sell has cost millions of investors many trillions of dollars in additional losses.

In 2008, most of the major stock market averages lost nearly 40% of their values. To make up for such losses and get back to even, you would need to have a more than 70% return in the following year. One-year returns like that will likely never happen, but many of the losses that investors took in 2008 could have been prevented had they simply eaten a slice of "humble pie." Right now, as you read this book, thousands of investors out there are holding onto stocks that they should have sold a long time ago. Whether they feel it's too late to sell, or got some advice that they'd be selling at the bottom, these investors are doing themselves a major disservice.

**The Bottom Line** is that by selling a losing position, you open up a door that could lead to a much better investing opportunity. Investors need to learn to embrace the word "sell;" not selling is the main error that causes investors (both short-term and long-term) to underperform. For some reason, investors tend to sell out of profitable positions and instead hold onto their underperforming stocks: This is an emblematic symptom of how investors have been taught to not sell by dollar cost averaging. Never be a deer in the headlights. Learn to accept selling as a critical part of the investing process!

# Stop-Loss Orders: A Tool Every Investor Should Utilize

If you have a brokerage account, you should utilize stop-loss orders. Regardless of your investment expertise, or amount of money you have invested, the stop-loss order is an important tool you can benefit from in a major way. Stop-loss orders are essential to successful investing by performing two key tasks:

- Protecting against further losses in losing positions
- Helping lock in gains on winning positions

A stop-loss order is a type of market order that automatically triggers when a stock reaches a certain price. You can activate your stop-loss order by logging onto your online brokerage account or calling your individual broker. For example, let's say you purchase a stock at $40 per share, and within one week the stock reaches $50 per share. If you're a short-term investor and want to protect the profits that you've achieved, you could place a stop-loss order for 10% below the high price, or $45. Thus, setting a stop-loss order for $45 per share will limit your loss from the stock's high to 10%, while protecting your gains. So, if the stock falls below $45 per share, your shares will automatically be sold. Thus, by utilizing stop-loss orders, you don't have to actively monitor how your individual stocks are performing on a daily basis. This is particularly important if you are in a situation that prevents you from checking on your stocks throughout the day or you are traveling for business or pleasure.

Investment commentators, analysts, and writers often overlook the importance stop-loss orders when discussing stock investing. Stop-loss orders are simple to activate and cost nothing to implement. You are charged only your regular commission by your broker when the stop-loss price has been reached and the stock is sold. Think of a stop loss as a free insurance policy to minimize losses—hopefully you never have to use it, but it's good to know you have protection in place in case you ever need it. Remember, there are no set rules at the price level you should set for your stop-loss order; it depends completely on your comfort level and investing style. An active trader may select 5%, whereas a long-term investor may prefer 15%, 20%, or even as much as 25% below the short-term target price. That's because in long-term investing, which is the way you'll become a Dividend Millionaire, day-to-day fluctuations aren't your true concern. Only major price movements that indicate a true shift in the viability of your holdings should cause you to liquidate your long-term positions.

There are two different types of stop-loss orders: limit orders and market orders. The difference between these two is important. **When placing your stop-loss order, it is essential that you select "market order" and not a "limit order."** With a "limit order," you take the risk that your order may not be filled if the market skips over your exact order price per share. For example, let's say you place a "limit order" for $48 per share, but the market is moving quickly, your stock's price could dart right through $48. If this scenario plays out, you may still own the stock, even though the stock is now below $48 and you had an active stop-loss order in place! When you contact your brokerage firm to inquire about your unfilled stop-loss order, your broker will likely tell you that the market moved fast and your order simply never got filled. Again, you can avoid this risk of your order not being filled if you select a market order" When you have a stop-loss market order, the minute your stocks hits $48 per share, your order automatically goes in, and you'll get the next best price. So, while you may not get out at *exactly* $48 per share, your stock will be sold somewhere close to that price—maybe at $47.90, or $47.60 per share, depending on how quickly the market moves and in what direction. Selecting a market order when using stop-losses is the only guarantee that your order will get filled.

After you choose the type of stop-loss order (always choose market order), you also need to select how long the stop-loss order remains active. Generally, you have two options: good for the day or good until canceled. Good until canceled means the order remains in place until it is activated on the day and time that your stock reaches the price you selected. In contrast, good for the day means your order is valid only until the end of the current market trading day. In most cases, I suggest using only good until canceled stop-loss orders. Good for the day orders can be useful, too, but I'd recommend those only in extreme situations and only for sophisticated investors.

Always remember, you can change and update your stop-loss order at any time you want—and you should! If your stock goes from $50 per share to $55 per share, and your original stop-loss was at $45 per share, you'll probably want to increase your stop-loss to somewhere around $52 per share. The stop-loss order is a great tool, but it isn't a free pass to simply forget about your holdings. You should still regularly monitor your portfolio, moving your stop-loss orders up as your stock's share price rises. This habit can continually enable you to lock in further gains as the stock continues to head higher.

When you are about to set up a stop-loss order for first time, I suggest having your broker walk you through the process over the phone. Give your account representative the name of the stock, its symbol, number of shares, and the price level you want to set the stop-loss order to be set at, and tell them you want the order "good until canceled. Also, have your representative show you how to check on your stop-loss orders to ensure they're activated and how to adjust them. If you have a full-service (not online) broker, have her email or fax you a confirmation to make sure she understood your exact instructions.

**The Bottom Line** is that if you want to sleep at night and avoid the gray hairs of worrying about the everyday ups and downs of the stock market, I believe using stop-loss orders is the way to go. Consider a stop-loss order as your insurance policy in case you can't watch the market or have an issue contacting your broker or connecting to your online account—it's your safety blanket in any kind of market.

It's human nature that people have a tough time of letting go of a losing position—we get emotionally involved with our stocks. A stop-loss enables you to make decisions without involving your emotions. You set up your disciplines and your rules so that you stay on track without clouding your judgment with emotions. Similar to how a safety gate prevents small children from tumbling down a set of stairs, your stop-loss can prevent your stock holdings from falling below the level you select. Remember, though, stop-losses don't mean your brokerage account is on autopilot. I want you to get into the habit at the end of each week of checking your account and looking at the individual transactions to confirm your actions were all carried out as you intended. It's easy to take for granted that you have entered your order correctly, when errors happen more frequently than you may think. Trust me, I've been there, and I'm the most methodical investor you'll ever meet! Review your transactions on a regular basis, and odds are you'll catch any mistakes before they cause any damage.

Finally, and I cannot stress this enough: The first time that you attempt a stop-loss order, have your broker or customer service rep of your online account walk you through the process. Then, when you fully understand and are comfortable with the process, you can take those training wheels off and do it yourself.

After you get your feet wet with a standard stop-loss order, you can then explore the trailing-stop strategy. Trailing stops are stop-loss orders that don't require you to set a specific price you'd like to sell at. Instead, you select either a dollar amount or percentage amount below the stock's high price, and your dollar amount or percentage "trails" the stock price as it moves up. For example, if you purchase Stock XYZ are $100 and immediately place a trailing stop sell order of $10, your sell-stop price will be $90. Let's say XYZ falls to a low of $91. In this case, your trailing stop order is not executed because XYZ hasn't fallen $10 from its high of $100. If the stock rises, however, your trailing stop rises along with it. Let's say XYZ jumps all the way up to $150; your trailing stop will be reset at $140, or $10 below the stock's high. As I mentioned earlier, you can also use percentages when setting trailing stops. If you set a 10% trailing stop on XYZ at $100, your stop-loss order would be triggered at $90. If XYZ rises to $150, however, your trailing stop won't trigger unless the price drops to $135, which is 10% lower than its high of $150. Thus, trailing stops prevent the need to continually log into your brokerage account and adjust your stop-loss orders as your holdings gain in value. Just as with standard stop-loss orders, though, **I urge you to have your broker or customer service rep walk you through the process first!**

# The Best Time to Sell and the Myth of Dollar Cost Averaging

As you learned in Chapter 5, "How to Find Winners and Avoid Losers," selling is a natural and essential part of the investing process. Too many times, you see investors that were sitting on big gains make a promise to themselves that they will never sell, no matter what. The "I'm in this for the long term" mentality kicks in, and many financial experts will sit right along side misguided investors during this counterproductive process. "Buy and hold" is a great strategy, especially with dividend-paying stocks, but that doesn't mean you should buy and hold *forever*, regardless of the circumstances!

Do you know why financial analysts and advisors love to hear people say, "I'm never selling"? It's simple: They want you to learn to accept losing positions because then they're off the hook if their advice turns out to be wrong. That's the unfortunate truth of the financial services industry. Few analysts or advisors are willing to take responsibility for bad calls they've made and therefore refuse to tell you to cut your losses before things get out of hand. It's important to remember that investment advisors are in the business of accumulating accounts. That's usually their #1 priority, whether they work for themselves or for larger firms. The reality is, advisors can't possibly run around all day opening accounts, while simultaneously watching the market, conducting research, and alerting clients about their individual holdings. There aren't enough hours in the day, and it's much easier for advisors to recommend what I feel is an inherently flawed practice called dollar cost averaging.

Dollar cost averaging is an investment strategy that entails transitioning into the market gradually by purchasing equal portions of a stock or mutual fund over the course of a year or more, regardless of the share price. The supposed advantage of buying a fixed dollar amount of a particular investment on a regular schedule is that the practice lessens the risk of investing a large amount in a single investment at the wrong time. Because you're investing the same dollar amount with each purchase, more shares are bought when prices are low, and fewer shares are bought when prices are high. Eventually, the average cost per share of the security will become smaller and smaller.

For example, let's say you decide to purchase $100 worth of Stock XYZ every month for three months. In January, XYZ is worth $33, so you buy three shares. In February, XYZ is worth $25, so you buy four shares this time. Finally, in March, XYZ is worth $20, so you buy five shares. In total, you would have purchased 12 shares for an average price of $25 each, as shown in Table 6.1.

**TABLE 6.1   An Example of Dollar Cost Averaging**

| Month | January | February | March | Total Investment |
|---|---|---|---|---|
| Shares | 3 shares at $33 | 4 shares at $25 | 5 shares at $20 | 12 shares at average of $25 |
| Cost | $100 | $100 | $100 | $300 |

In theory, this practice is supposed to limit your risk to market downturns because you're averaging your cost paid per share over the long term. Unfortunately, your upside potential in your investments is also limited because you're committing only a small amount of capital on a scheduled basis. On some recent tests we ran on Dividend.com, we found that in nearly two out of three 12-month investing periods, from 1950 to 2009 that investing a lump sum upfront would've provided better returns than dollar cost averaging each month. So why is it that so many fine upstanding financial experts sing the praises of dollar cost averaging? Maybe because it's an easy concept for advisors to use to keep their buy-and-hold investors pacified. If the market goes down, clients are told it's a great time to get "quality stocks at a cheap price." If the market goes up, everyone's happy, regardless of the stock price you'll be buying at. Simply put, your ability to generate the best returns possible is not through dollar cost averaging, and investing is about *results*, right? In the following chapters, I'm going to share with you my investing strategy that works in any market, bull or bear, and will help send you on your way to becoming a Dividend Millionaire.

Let me make something perfectly clear, though. I am not against investing a regular monthly amount in the market—that's a great way to start building a nest egg. The biggest reason I'm against dollar cost averaging is that it's a dumbed-down method of long-term investing. It requires you to buy the same stock over and over, regardless of share price or market conditions. To me, that's crazy! Buying more shares of a stock when the price is falling simply makes no sense. In most cases, there's a good reason behind why stock prices fall. It's like trying to catch a falling knife—you're usually going to get cut. If you're going to become a Dividend Millionaire, you need to focus on stocks that are on the way up, not down. With my method, I am going to train you to have the discipline to buy when stocks are going up and sell when stocks are going down, so you can shift your capital to a winning investment opportunity rather than continuing to put your funds into a sinking ship.

Using my method, you'll be trained to keep a portfolio that is loaded with stocks that are doing well and not ones that need to be nursed back to health. I want you to buy quality dividend-paying stocks first, and then when you feel comfortable and want to be a bit more aggressive (if ever), I want you to be looking at leaders in a growth space. Leaders in a growth space are companies growing their revenue 20% or more year over year.

Let's get back to selling. When investing over the long term, you should generally use a "down 20%" alert from the point of your average price per share. For example, if you own 100 shares of Stock XYZ at $75 per share, and the stock drops to around $60 a share (–20%), you should begin to consider selling the shares. Now, if the wider market is down altogether, and you think the setback is temporary, you can hold on a bit longer. However, if the price falls an additionally 10 percentage points from your average price per share (–30% total), it's time to kiss that stock goodbye! Remember, wide market meltdowns are rare, so there's probably a good reason your stock is falling so precipitously. And if the wider market *is* melting down, it's probably a good idea to sell anyway—you'll likely be presented with a better buying opportunity at a later date.

To figure out your average price per share, you simply divide your total cost of buying the shares by the number of shares you own. For example, If you've bought 100 shares of Stock XYZ at $70, another 100 shares at $75, and another 100 shares at $80, your average share cost is $75.

# Calculating Your Average Price Per Share

Total Cost of Purchasing Shares ÷ Number of Shares = **Average Price Per Share**

($700 + $750 + $800) ÷ 100 = **$75**

After you determine your average price per share, you can use that number to determine your 20% alert price—the point at which you should take a good look at potentially selling your stock. In the preceding example, the 20% alert price would be $60. When XYZ gets close to that level (which hopefully it never does!), it's time to consider saying goodbye. If it falls 30% from your average price per share, the decision has been made for you—sell the stock! You can use the chart in Table 6.2 to help you utilize the 20% alert method. Simply fill in each column of the chart, and you can easily track each stock you own in your portfolio. On my Dividend.com website, you can find an electronic version of this chart that you can access to track your holdings online.

**TABLE 6.2   Paul's 20% Sell Alert System**

| STOCK SYMBOL | NUMBER OF SHARES | AVERAGE PRICE | 20% ALERT TO WATCH | 30% SELL NOW | STOP LOSS? |
|---|---|---|---|---|---|
| | 100 | 40 | 32 | 28 | |
| | | | | | |
| | | | | | |

Now that you know my sell strategy when it comes to stocks that have lost value, let's move on to another important concept all investors should learn to embrace: profit taking. Profit taking simply refers to selling stocks you own that are up from when you bought them—taking a profit. Profit taking isn't all that important when in comes to dividend stock investing (which we cover in Chapter 7, "Dividend Stock Investing: The Only Long-Term Strategy That

Works"), but it's incredibly important when investing in growth stocks. Growth stocks are high-flying names that grow greatly in value over a relatively short amount of time. These names often attract large groups of momentum investors—short-term traders looking for quick gains who then head for the exits at the first sign of trouble. These traders can push a stock's value up significantly, but be ready to sell at a moment's notice, because growth stocks can fall just as quickly.

Selling at the absolute top of a stock's value is a pipe dream. No one ever successfully sells at the absolute top, except in cases of pure dumb luck. That's because it's impossible to tell when a stock will stop going up. On the other hand, you don't want to limit your gains by selling while a stock is still rising. So, how do we handle momentum stocks? The answer is simple: We *scale out* of them. Scaling out of a position is a simple practice that protects current profits, while keeping you exposed to further possible gains. Let's say you buy a stock at $20, and it heads to $40 within a matter of only six weeks. Normal stocks simply don't move that quickly, so it's obvious this is a growth stock with a whole lot of momentum investors jumping on board. The potential volatility (likelihood for the price to move quickly in either direction) for stocks like this is very high, so it's probably a good idea to begin scaling out of your position. Let's say you own 300 shares of this stock. To begin scaling out of your position, you could sell 100 shares and then wait to see what the stock does. If it continues higher, you could sell an additional 100 shares, and then finally, the last 100. This practice ensures that you capitalize on some of the stock's remaining run-up, without being as exposed to the risk of a quick drop-off.

Another sign you should sell a stock lies in a quickly rising dividend sign I watch for is when dividend yields get a bit too high (more than 8%) for certain sectors, namely financials. We witnessed many banks in 2008 that started sporting ultra-high dividend yields, only to later cut their dividend payouts to unsuspecting investors.

When it comes to dividend stocks, you usually do not get a tremendous amount of volatility unless they are stocks that are more of a high-growth play. For example, MasterCard (MA) has a small dividend yield (currently .40%), but it has far more growth potential than dividend plays in other sectors, such as utilities. I like to look at companies whose dividend yields make sense from a risk/reward standpoint. If I see stocks in the utility, energy, or **REIT** (Real Estate Investment Trust) sector whose dividend yields begin drop below 4%, it may be a sign that those particular stocks/sectors may be getting a bit too pricey.

A REIT is a security that trades like a stock and invests primarily in diverse real estate property holdings. Historically, investors have been attracted to this particular sector as a way to invest in real estate without everyday issues of being a landlord.

---

### Warning

We are beginning to see REITs change how their dividends are paid out. For example, Simon Property Group (SPG) recently announced a change in their payout structure. It will pay out most of its dividends in stock rather than cash. It will now pay a quarterly dividend of 9 cents per share of which 10 percent will be in cash and the rest in stock. SPG is hoping to save $925 million in cash in 2009 through this plan. As is the case of SPG, there are many other REITS that may actually follow in SPG footsteps. In the past, REITS have paid hefty dividends by distributing 90 percent of their taxable income in cash to shareholders, in exchange for not being taxed at the corporate level. Considering this latest announcement, you should be careful with REIT investing because we are now in unchartered waters, and it is best to be safe than sorry.

---

If more people had used the sell strategy I described earlier, many could have prevented a big chunk of the losses they experienced in the

tumultuous market of 2008—or any other poor stock market environments. Always remember that selling is a natural part of investing.
Buying is easy; anyone can do that. The art of when to sell is usually
the hardest thing for many investors to master.

**The Bottom Line** is that regardless of what price level you
bought a stock at, any time one of your holdings drops 20% to 30%,
you'd better have your finger ready to push the Sell button. I don't
care if it's a quality stock, or how well it's has performed for you in the
past. Ask any long-term General Motors, Fannie Mae, or Freddie
Mac investor how well the buy-and-never-sell strategy worked for
them—these stocks all went to just about $0! So remember, if you're
going to become a Dividend Millionaire, you need to learn to sell.
For example, say you bought General Electric at $10 per share, ten
years ago, and over the years it has steadily gone up to $40 per share.
Suddenly the stock market begins to correct and GE pulls back to $32
per share, which is exactly 20% off the $40 per share high. You as an
investor feel loyal to the stock; after all you bough it at $10 per share.
But stocks are not man's best friend; it's a piece of paper that sometimes you should hold and sometimes you need to get rid of. So in this
example with GE pulling back to $32 per share (20% down), your
next step alarm should be to examine the stock more closely. You
should ask yourself, "Is the stock price decline company-specific? Is
the market going through a correction?" So you need to decide that if
a stock drops 20%, how much lower does it go before you decide to
sell. If you are an investor that likes to give it some more rope, give it
some more time, I would not go another 10% past that point (which
would take us to the $28 level). A stock that has dropped 30% from
it's 52-week high—regardless of how well the company has performed in the past—you need to sell—sell—sell. Chances are the
stock or market is going though a correction, and you are probably sitting there doing nothing when you should actually be cutting your
loses.

# "This Time It's Different" Usually Means It's Time to Sell Soon

The two most recent bubbles in stock market history illustrate an important point: Don't ever get caught telling yourself, "This time it's different" when prices begin to break down. In the late 1990s, we had market experts telling investors that we were entering a new paradigm with the Internet and that valuing stocks needed to be looked at differently. Analysts everywhere were talking about "eyeballs" and "traffic" in relation to how they would factor a target price on a stock. Many market-watchers point to the Henry Blodgett (Merrill Lynch analyst) $400 price target he placed on Amazon.com in October 1998, as an ultimate sign of the tech market's mania. The stock was trading at less than $200 at the time, which some considered to already be extremely overvalued. Within weeks, the stock got to that $400 level and we were off to the races. The dot-com boom ran for almost 18 months beyond that before inevitably crashing back down. What investors didn't realize was that investment bankers were making a fortune bringing Internet IPOs, or new stock offerings, for companies that made no money at the time to the market.

Fast forward to 2006–2007, when real estate was in everyone's favorite graces, and we were "running out of land." Home flipping was all the rage, and many people deeply leveraged themselves to take advantage of the low interest rates. We all know what happened by 2008, and we are all feeling the disastrous after-effects from the lack of oversight from real estate and mortgage professionals.

**The Bottom Line** is that investment manias don't last forever. The real estate boom was supposed to last for decades, as many had promised; however, the market eventually ran out of immediate buyers. Crude Oil is another area that recently saw a buying mania take hold. When oil prices jumped to nearly $150 a barrel, many expected the $200 level to arrive not long after. Not even six months after almost touching $150, oil prices fell all the way back down to $40 a barrel. Manias like these will always pop up over time, and they all end the same way. Investors need to be aware where the manias started and how far they have run before believing any of the rhetoric that you may hear from those that have a lot at stake to keep the bubbles inflating. When you recognize a bubble beginning to burst, you know what to do: Sell!

# Losing Investments Can Be a Good Thing!

The title of this chapter may seem confusing, but as an old baseball coach once told me, "You always learn more from your losses than you do from your wins." One of the things that helps me be a consistent performer in the markets was my ability to go back and learn about where and why I made my mistakes. In the sporting world, many athletes do this by watching the films of their performances. In investing, it's simply a matter of just taking the time and looking at your wins and losses in your log book.

To succeed in investing, you need to think like a professional athlete. Successful athletes would never show up for a game without knowing their play book. Similarly, you need to regularly check your play book to track how you are performing. At least once a month, I want you to enter your performance into your log book, so you learn from your past mistakes just like your favorite athlete would. I have listed an example of a log book in Table 6.3, so fill in this chart and track your portfolio at least once a month. On my website, Dividend-Millionaire.com, you can find an electronic version of this chart.

**TABLE 6.3 Example Investing Log Book**

| Share # | Stock Name/Symbol | Date Acquired | Date Sold | Price Purchased | Price Sold | Gain (Loss) |
|---------|-------------------|---------------|-----------|-----------------|------------|-------------|
|         |                   |               |           |                 |            |             |
|         |                   |               |           |                 |            |             |
|         |                   |               |           |                 |            |             |

**The Bottom Line** is that in investing, as in any profession, there is always a need to figure out where your potential weaknesses may be and what are the things you can do to avoid making similar investing mistakes. You'd be surprised at what bad tendencies you can recognize just by examining your losing investments. Remember, human nature dictates that we tend to repeat the same mistakes over and over again. It happens not only in the markets but also in personal life decisions. The key is to learn from your mistakes by taking the time to examine the causes of your bad decisions.

# 7

## Dividend Stock Investing: The Only Long-Term Strategy That Works

### Eventually the Turtle Always Beats the Hare—Slow and Steady Returns Build Dividend Millionaires!

Many investors start out with good intentions about setting money aside for retirement. What often happens, however, is the discipline and consistency needed for successful investing unfortunately takes a back seat to quick profits and risky market bets. This chapter reveals all the key information you'll ever need to know about the single, best long-term investment option available: dividend-paying stocks. Investors need to be aware of several factors to consistently pick high-quality dividend stocks, so let's stick to the basics first.

### What Exactly Is a Dividend?

Before you begin investing, you need to know how a dividend stock differs from a nondividend stock. For every share of a **dividend stock** that you own, you periodically receive a portion of the company's earnings in the form of a *dividend payout*—funds the company pays shareholders simply for owning the stock. The two main types of dividend payouts are **cash dividends** and **stock dividends**. The most common are **cash dividends**, which are cash payments made to stockholders out of the company's current earnings or accumulated profits. Stocks that do not pay dividends count solely on price appreciation (capital gains) for investment returns, whereas dividend stocks can provide the highly advantageous combination of income (periodic cash payouts in the form of dividends) *and* capital gains. Each company sets its own dividend policy, and although some have paid dividends for decades (such as AT&T), other companies have never paid dividends and probably never will (such as Google).

Let's use a popular dividend stock as an example of how cash dividend payouts work. In 2008, Kraft Foods (KFT) paid an annualized cash dividend of $1.16 per share. Like most U.S.-based companies that pay dividends, Kraft makes its payouts on a quarterly basis (four times a year), so at the end of each fiscal quarter, the company sent a payment for one quarter of $1.16 (29 cents) for each share a stockholder owned. As an investor in a dividend stock, you must decide how you want this cash dividend to be paid to you. There are two options available: You can either receive the dividend check or have the dividends automatically reinvested back into more shares of the stock in the form of a Dividend ReInvestment Plan (DRIP). We'll talk more about DRIPs and the compounding returns they can provide in a later section, but if you are of retirement age, you may depend on the dividend payouts as part of your income and therefore will probably prefer to receive a check. If you not retired, however, I recommend you put your dividends to work by reinvesting them into more shares.

The other main type of dividend payout method is a **stock dividend**. A stock dividend distributes additional shares of stock to shareholders rather than cash. Sometimes, companies present stock dividends to shareholders in lieu of their normal cash dividend during times when money is tight. If a company lacks the cash on hand to cover its cash dividend payouts, it might instead issue additional shares of stock to its investors. In these cases, any fractional shares left over from the stock dividend must be paid out as cash because companies can't issue partial shares.

Now that we know exactly what a dividend is, and have discussed the two types of dividend payouts, it's time to debunk a common myth about investing. Many people believe that it takes a large sum of money to get started investing in the stock market—this simply isn't true. You can find several brokerages out there today, such as Share-Builder for example, that enable you to invest as little as $25 a week, and even offer the opportunity to pool your money with other investors to buy fractional shares of stocks. This may not seem like a lot of money, but after you've built your portfolio up to thousands of shares, and consistently use dividends to buy more stock in solid companies, you can easily make a great deal of money over the long term. Check out this example of just how effective this strategy can be.

> If you invested a mere $50 per month—that's $600 per year—in dividend stocks from the age of 8 to 13, and reinvested those dividends, you will have accumulated more than $1 million by the time you reach the age of 65.[*]

Now *that's* how you become a Dividend Millionaire!

**The Bottom Line** is that the old saying that "It takes money to make money" may hold true in many situations, but dividend stocks are certainly one exception to that rule. As illustrated in the preceding example, a mere $50 per month for a five-year period can grow into a nest egg of more than one million dollars over the course of several decades. Here is the one steadfast rule to observe, however: After you start to invest, you need to keep investing and be methodical and consistent with your investment choices. I am not asking you to dollar cost average (especially in a down market)—I am simply recommending you stay disciplined and invest on a regular basis. I want you to make investing part of your daily or weekly regimen. You

---

[*] Based on historic 11% annual return rate for dividend-paying stocks with dividends reinvested.

keep your body healthy and strong each day with daily tasks such as brushing your teeth and taking vitamins, right? Take the same care with your investment portfolio by investing and monitoring your investments on a daily or weekly basis, as well. We have long since left the era of buy-and-hold (or to be more precise, buy-and-never-sell), so you need to stay alert and proactive to keep your investments healthy.

## The Beauty of Compounding Returns and Why It Doesn't Take Much Money to Start

As noted earlier, dividend-paying stocks have averaged an 11% annual return over the past 75 years. Let's use some examples of how your dollar amounts can grow over the various time periods using 11% as the expected return. Say you started with $1,000 and invested in some quality dividend stocks. Without putting any more money into your investment, using a compounding rate calculator, we can estimate that your $1,000 after 10 years would be worth $2,839.44. After 20 years, your total would be $8,062.35. Finally, after 30 years, your original $1,000 would be worth $22,892.41. That's nearly a 2,300% return on investment!

That isn't nearly enough to retire on, but that example entailed only a single $1,000 investment without adding another penny. Let's say you invested $50,000 instead without any additional investment. After the same 30-year period, your portfolio would be worth $1.144 million—now we're talking! Of course, you don't need to invest $50,000 or even $1,000 to start in dividend investing, though. These are just a couple of scenarios to show just how big your returns can be if you invest in quality dividend-paying stocks over the course of time. If you stay the course, dividend stocks have the track record to get the job done for any investor. Let's look at another well-known example.

Back in 1980, if you had invested $2,000 in PepsiCo (PEP) stock, your investment would have reached to more than $150,000 by the end of 2004. You would have started with just 80 shares, but by reinvesting dividends, you now would have accumulated 2,800 shares over the course of nearly 25 years. Similarly, if you had $2,000 invested in Philip Morris (now called Altria) stock in 1980, by the end of 2004, the net worth of your portfolio would have reached just under $300,000. That is with just getting started with 58 shares. Over the course of time and the dividends being raised and reinvested, you would be the owner of more than 4,300 shares!

Are you a dividend believer yet? Dividend-paying stocks are clearly the way to go for any long-term investor. The only essential components are **reinvesting your dividends** while **not straying from your investment plan**.

**The Bottom Line** is that with even a little bit of money, you can truly make your dreams a reality as long as you stick to a plan and systematically and methodically invest and reinvest those dividends. The beauty of reinvesting dividends is that you accumulate more and more shares over time without outlaying any additional capital. These compounding returns, when combined with long-term price appreciation, make for a powerful foundation to build a fortune upon—that's how you can become a Dividend Millionaire.

# The All-Important Dividend Dates

Usually on a quarterly basis, each company's board of directors determines what size and type of dividend should be distributed, if any. *Please note that no public company is required to pay a dividend, regardless of its past dividend history, or even if it has already announced its next payout amount and payment date.* Most companies in good financial standing are dedicated to maintaining (and often increasing) their dividend payouts, however, so they are reluctant to reduce or stop paying dividends unless absolutely necessary. Dividends are normally paid on a regular schedule, and you need to be aware of four essential dates:

- **Declaration date**—This is the date on which the board of directors announces to shareholders and the market as a whole that the company intends to pay a dividend. On this day, the company provides three more dates that pertain to the payout.

- **Ex-date (Ex-dividend date)**—This is the single most important date in the dividend investing world. On or after the ex-dividend date, a stock no longer comes attached with the right to be paid the most recently declared dividend. In other words, **you must purchase a stock *before* its ex-dividend date to receive its next scheduled dividend payout.** The ex-dividend date is important for the company, as well, because it makes reconciliation of who is to be paid the dividend easier. Prior to the ex-dividend date, the stock is said to be *cum dividend* ("with dividend"): Existing holders of the stock and anyone who buys it will receive the dividend, whereas any holders selling the stock lose their right to the dividend. On and after this date the stock becomes *ex-dividend* ("without dividend"): Existing holders of the stock *will* receive the dividend even if they now sell the stock, whereas anyone who now buys the stock now will not receive the dividend. In almost all cases, the ex-dividend date falls two days before the record date.

- **Date of record (record date)**—This is the date on which the company physically looks at its records to see who the shareholders of the company are. Shareholders who properly registered their ownership on or before the date of record (normally determined by the ex-dividend date) will receive the dividend. Shareholders who are not registered as of this date will not receive the dividend. Registration in most countries is essentially automatic for shares purchased before the ex-dividend date. In almost all cases, the record date falls two business days after the ex-dividend date.

- **Payment date (payable date)**—The payment date, also known as the payable date, is the day when the dividend checks will actually be mailed to the shareholders of a company or credited to brokerage accounts. This date may be several weeks after the date of record so that the company can accurately confirm the payout to the shareholders of record.

What's the point of all these dividend dates? Well, ex-dividend dates were created to make sure the dividend checks go the right shareholders and not individuals trying to beat the system. It takes three business days from the transaction date for the stock purchase to be entered into the company's record books. If you are not in the company's record book on the date of record, you won't receive the dividend payout. So, if you want to receive the dividend, you need to have purchased the stock at least three business days before the date of record—one day *before* the ex-dividend date. To further illustrate this point, look at Table 7.1. If you buy on the ex-dividend date (Tuesday), which is only two business days before the date of record, you will not receive a dividend because your name will not appear in the company's record book until Friday. If you want to sell the stock and still receive the dividend, you need to sell on or after the ex-dividend date (Tuesday).

**TABLE 7.1   Dividend Date Example**

| Buy on This Date to Receive Dividend | Ex-Dividend Date | | Record Date | |
|---|---|---|---|---|
| Monday | Tuesday | Wednesday | Thursday | Friday |
| 1st | 2nd | 3rd | 4th | 5th |

**The Bottom Line** is that new investors to the dividend market almost always try to beat the system. They try to buy a stock, receive the dividend, and then dump the stock within the same day or day after the ex-dividend date. What many new investors fail to realize, however, is that stock exchanges negatively (and automatically) adjusts each stock the ex-dividend date day so that the stock reflects the dividend being paid out. The stock's price decreases on the ex-dividend date by an amount roughly equal to the dividend paid. This reflects the decrease in the company's assets resulting from the declaration of the dividend and was put in place to prevent people from gaming the dividend system. The company does not take any explicit action to adjust its stock price; in an efficient market, buyers and sellers automatically price this in. For example, let's say that Microsoft's quarterly payout is 25 cents, and its ex-dividend date is on Tuesday. On Monday, the stock closed out at $20 per share. On Tuesday, when the stock opens to trading, it is not going to open at $20 per share but $19.75 per share. That new share price is the stock trading ex-dividend ("without dividend"). I like to tell investors to call their broker and find out how the broker handles for the dividend payouts, because each broker may handle the day the transaction clears in a different way. Regardless, you should remember what these important dates mean and avoid trying to find a trading edge when it comes to dividends. It usually doesn't work and it is not the reason why you should be looking to buy and invest in dividend stocks.

## Dividend Yields and Avoiding Potential Dividend Traps

A huge factor when considering dividend stocks is *dividend yield*. A stock's dividend yield refers to the amount of annual return you can expect in terms of dividend payouts in relation to its share price. So, to calculate a stock's dividend yield, simply divide the annual dividend by the current stock price. An example: If company XYZ trades for $20 per share and pays a $1 annualized dividend, using our formula (Annual Dividend ÷ Current Stock Price = Dividend Yield), we find the answer is 5%.

> How to Calculate Dividend Yield
> Annual Dividend ÷ Current Stock Price = Dividend Yield
> Example:
> $1 ÷ $20 = 5%

When investing manias fade and bubbles burst, we see numerous situations where stocks have fallen so far that they are sporting abnormally high dividend yields. (Because if dividend payouts remain constant, lower stock prices means higher yields.) On the surface, these yields look attractive, but for many of them, they represent nothing more than dividend traps. Many companies whose prices fall precipitously over a short period of time do not address the dividend payout status until their quarterly earnings report and often may insist that they will continue to pay out dividends at the same level. We have seen even large, well-known companies such as Bank of America and Citigroup defend the strength of their financial assets and insist the dividend is not in any danger, only to later cut the dividend. At Dividend.com, the research we do has spotted many of these "dividend traps," and we've maneuvered successfully through several of these scenarios.

The best rule of thumb is to focus on stocks whose dividend yields range from 3% to 10%. (And even 10% may be too high in some cases.)

I like to investigate the high yield names and figure out why the yields are so high, outside of just a drop in the stock price. There will be times in which the selling in a particular stock gets overdone, and the company can bounce back with little long-term damage that has hurt the fundamentals of the company. We can use McDonald's (MCD) situation in 2003 and Altria Group's (MO) situation from 1999 as some well-known examples of when the market gave investors a major buying opportunity. Those investors that bought back then and have held onto these names are looking at stocks yielding double-digit dividend yields each year, after factoring the dividend increases each of the companies declared since then.

Another tool investors can look at to determine if the dividend can be sustained is to look at a stock's *payout ratio*. Payout ratio is the amount of earnings paid out in dividends to shareholders. The lower the ratio, the more secure the dividend because smaller dividends are easier to pay out than larger dividends. If company XYZ earned $2 per diluted share last quarter and paid out $1 per share in dividends, it would have a payout ratio of 50% because it paid out half of its income as dividends to shareholders.

How to Calculate Payout Ratio

Payout Ratio = Dividends per Share ÷ Earnings per Share

So, in our example (MSFT)...

$1 ÷ $2 = 0.5, or a 50% Payout Ratio

This example is a healthy payout ratio. The company is issuing a solid amount of its income to shareholders, while banking the other half to grow its business and its share price.

A payout ratio of more than 75% is where we begin to get concerned. Certain stocks, such as REITs, however, are an exception to this rule. REITs (Real Estate Investment Trusts) are federally required to pay out a minimum of 90% of their taxable profits in the form of dividends. We have witnessed the recent real estate collapse hurt many different area of the REIT sector, but I avoided much of the carnage by sticking to the strict sell disciplines that I talked about in the previous chapters. When a stock that I am invested in drops 20%, my inner alarm goes off, and I dig further into why that has occurred. In a four-month period in 2008, many of the best and largest well-known REIT plays dropped anywhere from 50% to 80% from their 52-week highs, whereas 38 of the 111 REITs we followed cut or suspended their dividends. The ones that didn't cut their dividends sported juicy dividend yields. Unfortunately, it was only a matter of time before those dividends were slashed as well because their share prices had fallen so significantly. Why hold a stock that pays a 6% dividend yield but then goes down 50%, 60%, or 70%? It will take a significant amount of time for the share price to recover back to those levels (if at all!). This is yet another example in which a sell strategy can never hurt you. It may be a sign that the company does not have much growth in the near future. A payout ratio of 100% or higher is usually a sure sign that a dividend cut is around the corner because it indicates a company is actually losing money by paying out more money to shareholders than it is bringing in. Many of these types of stocks tend to trade under $5 per share. I almost always avoid shares at those levels, and I believe investors looking to become Dividend Millionaires should probably even avoid all stocks trading at under $10 per share.

**The Bottom Line** is that you should not get enamored with high dividend yield stocks without knowing the details of why they are sporting those high yields! You'll save yourself from making a lot of bad investments. Rather than looking at a company that has a high dividend yield and thinking that is the way to go, do your research to determine how they got there. Always be on the lookout for "dividend traps"—stocks having a dividend yield of 10% and above are usually risky investments.

# Look for Dividend Stocks from Companies That Continue to Raise Their Dividends on a Regular Basis

An important strategy in picking quality dividend stocks is to focus on recent *dividend history*. Companies that have consistently raised their dividend payouts each year demonstrate a dedication to their long-term investors and are highly unlikely to cut their dividends in the future. On Dividend.com, my team has helped assemble a list of companies that have increased their annualized dividend payout for 25 consecutive years. We update this list each year, removing names that have failed to boost their payouts and sometimes adding new names that qualify. Here is our 25-Year Dividend Increasers list, as of December 31, 2009:

1. Diebold (DBD) (57)
2. American States Water (AWR) (55)
3. Dover (DOV) (54)
4. Genuine Parts (GPC) (54)
5. Northwest Natural Gas (NWN) (54)
6. Procter & Gamble (PG) (53)
7. Emerson Electric (EMR) (53)
8. 3M (MMM) (52)
9. Parker Hannifin Corporation (PH) (52)
10. Integrys Energy Group (TEG) (51)

11. Vectren Corp (VVC) (50)

12. Cincinnati Financial (CINF) (49)

13. Coca-Cola Co. (KO) (48)

14. Johnson & Johnson (JNJ) (47)

15. Colgate-Palmolive (CL) (47)

16. Lowe's (LOW) (47)

17. Lancaster Colony Corp. (LANC) (47)

18. Nordson Corp (NDSN) (46)

19. Illinois Tool Works (ITW) (45)

20. Chubb Corp (CB) (45)

21. Hormel Foods (HRL) (44)

22. Tootsie Roll (TR) (44)

23. ABM Industries (ABM) (43)

24. California Water Services Group (CWT) (43)

25. SJW Corp (SJW) (43)

26. Stanley Black & Decker, Inc. (SWK) (42)

27. Eli Lilly (LLY) (42)

28. Federal Realty Investment Trust (FRT) (42)

29. Target (TGT) (42)

30. Commerce Bankshares (CBSH) (42)

31. Stepan Co. (SCL) (42)

32. Sysco Corp (SYY) (40)

33. Black Hills Corp (BKH) (40)

34. H.B. Fuller Co. (FUL) (40)

35. Connecticut Water Services (CTWS) (40)

36. National Fuel Gas (NFG) (39)

37. Universal Corp (UVV) (39)

38. Kimberly-Clark (KMB) (38)

39. Abbott Labs (ABT) (38)

**40.** PPG Industries (PPG) (38)

**41.** W.W.Grainger (GWW) (38)

**42.** C.R. Bard, Inc. (BCR) (38)

**43.** Leggett & Platt (LEG) (38)

**44.** Washington Real Estate Investment Trust (WRE) (38)

**45.** Tennant Co. (TNC) (38)

**46.** Wesco Financial (WSC) (38)

**47.** V.F. Corporation (VFC) (37)

**48.** McGraw-Hill (MHP) (37)

**49.** PepsiCo (PEP) (37)

**50.** Becton Dickinson (BDX) (37)

**51.** Centurytel Inc. (CTL) (37)

**52.** Nucor Corp (NUE) (37)

**53.** Helmerich Payne (HP) (37)

**54.** Middlesex Water Co. (MSEX) (37)

**55.** Mine Safety Applications (MSA) (37)

**56.** Consolidated Edison (ED) (36)

**57.** RPM International (RPM) (36)

**58.** Telephone & Data Systems (TDS) (36)

**59.** United Bankshares (UBSI) (36)

**60.** Wal-Mart Stores (WMT) (35)

**61.** Automatic Data Processing (ADP) (35)

**62.** Archer Daniels Midland Co. (ADM) (35)

**63.** Gorman-Rupp (GRC) (35)

**64.** RLI Corp (RLI) (35)

**65.** Walgreen Co. (WAG) (34)

**66.** Sigma-Aldrich Corporation (SIAL) (34)

**67.** Family Dollars Stores (FDO) (34)

**68.** MGE Energy (MGEE) (34)

69. Pentair Inc. (PNR) (34)

70. McDonald's (MCD) (33)

71. Carlisle Co. (CSL) (33)

72. WGL Holdings (WGL) (33)

73. Clorox Co. (CLX) (32)

74. Sherwin Williams (SHW) (32)

75. Medtronic (MDT) (32)

76. Piedmont Natural Gas (PNY) (32)

77. Teleflex (TFX) (31)

78. Bank of Hawaii (BOH) (30)

79. Questar Corp (STR) (30)

80. Eaton Vance (EV) (29)

81. Franklin Resources (BEN) (29)

82. Old Republic (ORI) (29)

83. Valspar Corp (VAL) (29)

84. Energen Corp (EGN) (28)

85. Pitney Bowes (PBI) (28)

86. Community Trust Bancorp (CTBI) (28)

87. Weyco Group (WEYS) (28)

88. Aflac (AFL) (27)

89. Air Products & Chemicals (APD) (27)

90. Bemis Co. (BMS) (27)

91. Cintas (CTAS) (27)

92. Exxon Mobil (XOM) (27)

93. AT&T (T) (26)

94. Clarcor (CLC) (26)

95. Brown-Forman (BF-B) (26)

96. BancorpSouth (BXS) (25)

You'll probably instantly recognize many of these companies because several of them have been top brands for several decades. Many big-time financial and manufacturing names *used* to appear on this list, such as Bank of America, Citigroup, General Electric, and so on but have since cut their dividends significantly amid the economic turmoil that has defined the past few years in the markets. Certain companies, however, such as Coca-Cola (KO), Procter & Gamble (PG), Johnson & Johnson (JNJ), and PepsiCo are firmly cemented on this list. Let's look at some of the historical dividend charts of those four companies (see Figure 7.1).

In contrast to the great stocks previously shown, we tend to shy away from companies whose dividend growth becomes stagnant; this can sometimes be the tip-off sign that profit growth may be beginning to wane. We've witnessed newspaper companies, radio companies, and others in essentially dying industries plus other areas of the market that have seen technology and other innovations stem their historic revenue growth streams.

Let's look at what happened to a company like *The New York Times* (NYT), as shown in Figure 7.2.

Now, look at the same stock's historical dividend chart for the same time period, as shown in Figure 7.3.

*The New York Times* is the poster child for what can happen to a stock that does not adapt to the effects technology has on an industry's landscape. As the company fell further and further behind other media giants during the online content revolution, its stock price quickly declined. Amid that share price decline, it became increasingly likely that the company would be forced to slash its dividend payout. *The New York Times* did just that in November 2008, lowering its payout from 23 cents quarterly to just 6 cents. Then, in the following quarter, the company eliminated its dividend entirely!

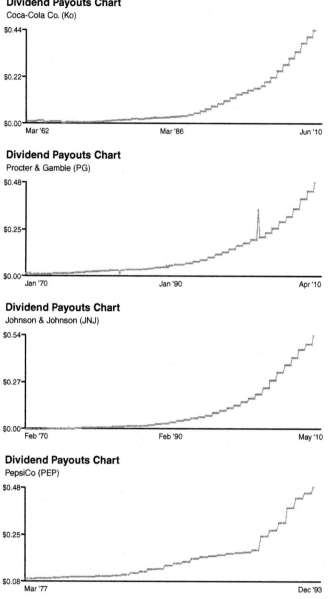

**Dividend Payouts Chart**
Coca-Cola Co. (Ko)

**Dividend Payouts Chart**
Procter & Gamble (PG)

**Dividend Payouts Chart**
Johnson & Johnson (JNJ)

**Dividend Payouts Chart**
PepsiCo (PEP)

Figure 7.1   Historical dividend charts

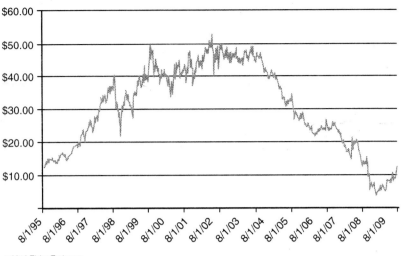

**Figure 7.2 The New York Times (NYT)**

## Dividend Payouts Chart

(NYT)

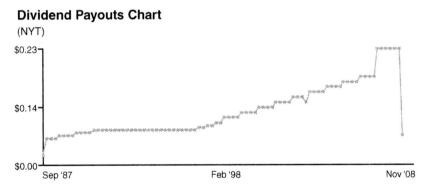

**Figure 7.3 Historical dividend chart for the New York Times (NYT)**

**The Bottom Line** is that simply put, the best long-term investments are dividend stocks in solid sectors with a good recent history of increasing their dividends. Remember, companies will boost their payouts only if business is good and they are turning consistent profits. When a company stops raising its dividends, it should be a flashing yellow light to be cautious. For example, at the end of 2008, Pfizer (PFE) for the first time in over a decade said it would not raise its dividend payout for the following year. Just one quarter after that, Pfizer slashed its payout in half! Now, companies with consistent dividends aren't guaranteed to see their share prices go up in value, but rising dividends are certainly a good sign—especially in tough economies.

# The Dangers of "Value" or "Cheap" Dividend Stocks

Whether you buy individual stocks or even mutual funds, one of the things you need to be aware of is the myth that *value investing* is a sound investing strategy. As soon as markets crater, investors begin looking for "safe" stocks. For years, I watched the endless parade of fund managers appear on TV preaching about the safety net of buying cheap stocks. Then they would showcase their list of recommended names, and I would get sick to my stomach. Over and over again, these jerks would recommend stocks such as Alcoa (AA), which went on to slash its dividend by 82% in 2009 General Motors (GM), which eliminated its dividend and subsequently went bankrupt in that same year, and REIT plays such as General Growth Properties (GGP), which suspended its dividend in 2008. Sometimes I wondered if these managers had a clue of what trends were playing out in the real world. The worst part of watching them peddle the same names over and over again was that a sell strategy seemed to be nonexistent. The we're-in-this-for-the-long-haul mantra was the consistent cop-out, and business reporters never seemed to push these hucksters for real answers.

The market is littered with many other "value" plays that simply have continued to crash and burn—companies such as Eastman Kodak (EK), Xerox (XRX), Corning (GLW), and Nortel Networks (NT), just to name a few. Let's look at the case of Nortel Networks specifically. Nortel was a company that during the peak of the technology boom of the late 90s had nearly 100,000 employees and a market cap of nearly $300 billion. This one-mighty tech giant never recovered from its downward spiral, despite that many fund managers claimed it would, and on January 14, 2009, the company filed for bankruptcy protection.

Investors should be wary of trying to catch these so-called "value plays." I have said this many times in various articles and newsletters that I've written: In most cases, it holds true that **cheap stocks aren't good because good stocks aren't cheap.** Sure, bull markets are great for most investors, but sometimes the markets are just plain going to go down. It's simply part of the natural economic cycle. In contrast to what many would have you believe, the economy won't turn back around overnight. Unfortunately, during these situations, the business media loves saying things like "This is the greatest buying opportunity we've ever seen," or "Buy when there's blood in the streets."

One data point that tends to fool investors and fund managers alike is a company's P/E ratio (Price-to-Earnings, commonly referred to as "P to E"). This ratio is calculated by dividing the stock's current share price by the company's earnings per share made over a 12-month time period. Let's say company XYZ's share price is $40 and their earnings for 2008 were $4 per share. The PE ratio in this case would be 10.

P/E RATIO = Current Share Price ÷ Earnings Per Share
Example:
10 = $40 ÷ $4

"Value" investors tend to gravitate toward low P/E ratios to find cheap stocks. The danger of this strategy lies in that P/E doesn't get recalculated until a company's next earnings report. As a stock's share price declines, its P/E declines, too, and investors get lulled into a false sense of security that they're buying a name that is undervalued— until its earnings report comes out with weak future guidance, its price plummets, and the investors realize they made a big mistake.

We witnessed this phenomenon in the past few years with home-building stocks. We saw some homebuilders with P/E's of 5 or 6, which seemingly indicated that they were undervalued and poised for a run-up. Investors were led to believe that these stocks were "cheap" in relation to their PE values. However, the housing market was entering a historical cyclical decline, and those stocks were bound to see much lower future earnings. Further price drops and dividend cuts or outright suspensions were soon to follow. So, when a PE ratio is below 6, be aware that the company's growth is probably yesterday's news.

**The Bottom Line** is that investors should know that sometimes bad news is just bad news. Simply put, buying every dip in a bear market is a recipe for disaster. Markets usually overshoot on the upside and the downside, so the only way to know the bottom is when market values are at least 20% to 25% above the market lows for a sustained period of time. (Four to six months is probably a good area to start with.) The market is extremely good at determining stock values, and in most cases, there are several good reasons why a stock's value is lower than you may think it "should" be. Beware of P/E ratios in the mid-to-low single digits. Some investors gravitate toward low P/E ratio stocks because they feel they don't want to pay a lot for earnings. Always remember that, though, that some sectors are cyclical, such as housing and commodities. Within these sectors, the market is driven by cyclical forces that cause stocks to rise or fall over relatively brief periods of time. As a rule of thumb, when P/E ratios are extremely low, most of the time the company is about to top off before earnings fall off a cliff.

# DARS™ (Dividend Advantage Ratings System)

As a market fanatic, I wanted to develop my own system to determine which dividend stocks investors should consider for their portfolios. I was in the "lab" with my team for several months formulating what I felt would be a great foundation for investment criteria. After studying some of the well-known techniques that have worked during different cycles, and some that didn't work during other periods, I put together a comprehensive ratings system to find high-yielding dividend stocks that will outperform in good markets, and perhaps more important, avoid the carnage of the bear markets.

I named my system DARS™, or Dividend Advantage Rating System, and these are the five major criteria I use to rate and rank stocks:

- **Relative strength**—Indicates whether the stock is uptrending. One major determining factor in this rating is whether the stock is trading above its 50- and 200-day moving averages.
- **Overall yield attractiveness**—Reflects our personal opinion about a stock's capability to continue to make its current dividend payout. High dividend yields (usually more than 10%) should be considered extremely risky, whereas low dividend yields (1% or less) are simply not beneficial to long-term investors.
- **Dividend reliability**—Determined by the number of years the company has been paying dividends. The longer a company has been reliably paying dividends, the higher its rating.
- **Dividend uptrend**—Dependent on the company's history of regularly increasing its cash dividends.
- **Earnings growth**—Indicates a company's projected earnings for the next four quarters. Stock price is usually tied to earnings growth, and companies also use earnings projections to determine their dividend policy.

I give each stock on Dividend.com a score of 1 (lowest) to 5 (highest) for each of these criteria and then average out the score to determine its overall DARS™ rating. Figure 7.4 shows the breakdown of my DARS™ scores and what they mean.

**The Bottom Line** is that I hope that many of you who read this book consider paying a visit to Dividend.com (if you haven't done so already) to see for yourself what years of hard work and tremendous effort have built. I believe our Web site is a great way for any investor

## How to Interpret Dividend.com Ratings

Each dividend stock receives one of four basic classifications based upon its Overall Rating:

| Overall Rating | Classification | Explanation |
|---|---|---|
| 0.0 - 2.4 | Avoid for Now | Stock is not investable at the current time (also known as a "Sell"). |
| 2.5 - 3.4 | Neutral | Stock is considered a mediocre dividend-paying stock (also known as a "Hold"). |
| 3.5 - 3.7 | Recommended | Stock is a good dividend-paying stock to own at current levels (also known as a "Buy"). |
| 3.75 - 5 | Highly Recommended | Stock is an outstanding dividend-paying stock investment (also known as a "Strong Buy"). |

Remember, when we remove a name from our "Recommended" dividend stocks list, that downgrade generally means that we no longer recommended adding to existing positions, or establishing new positions in that stock. **All investors should develop their own sell strategies to limit losses.**

**Figure 7.4   My DARS™ scores**

to stay up to date with what is happening in the markets, especially anyone looking to find the best dividend stocks for their portfolios. This book with my efforts on Dividend.com, can help an investor remain on course to become a Dividend Millionaire!

# 8

# Trading Techniques and Pitfalls That All Investors Should Know

## Becoming a Full-Time Trader

One of the biggest decisions I ever made in my life was to sell the family food business that had provided my family (wife and daughter, later came another daughter and then a son) and I with financial freedoms and flexibility. Deciding to leave that consistent salary for what was a bit of an unproven track record was not something that would come without hesitation. I remember telling my wife that for me to become a full-time trader, one of the things I wanted to do was sell our home so that I could have an even bigger cushion to fall back on if I would struggle in my investing. It took a special woman to agree to such a request, but she knew how badly I wanted to make the foray into trading. I had some early success in trading before I even sold my business, but felt I could do even better if I could dedicate my full time and energy to the markets.

One of the key things to know if you want to become a successful full-time trader is that you need a good amount of capital. (I would say $250K is a good number to start with.) That way, you can use margin to gain up to $1 million in buying power for a trading day. In most cases, I don't recommend buying stock on margin, but it can enable you some much-needed room to maneuver in certain situations. The key to remember is that if you do use margin, be sure to end the day at your cash values at a minimum—this helps avoid any potential blow-ups that can occur when companies disseminate news after hours. Also, you need to make sure you have total support from your spouse if you are married. Life changes dramatically when you take the role of being a full-time stock trader. You need to be 100% dedicated and be prepared to use your time wisely. I went from being in the public eye seven days a week with my business to the isolation of being in my office/bedroom doing my own research every day. I also went from a 3,000-square-foot home to a 950-square-foot apartment!

When I began full-time trading, I worked out of my bedroom the entire day. My two young daughters would come into my room constantly, and this was something that as a dad, I grew accustomed to. I knew that the kids would want to check in with me whenever they wanted. There were times, though, that I had to tell my wife that I needed to hang the "Do Not Disturb" sign up, but that was usually when the markets were super-volatile or the market open was chaotic. I began to miss the limelight of being around people all day, but eventually that wore off as I began to get used to my new schedule. I went from getting up at 4:30 a.m. to head to open my food business to waking up at 5:30 a.m. to log on to my computer and prepare for the market day. I'd check what the overseas markets were doing and then get *The Wall Street Journal* and *Investors Business Daily*. As my trading career went on, my strategies kept evolving.

In the following sections, I'm going to let you in on my personal trading strategy that allowed me some great returns during my career. Just make sure you are prepared to make the sacrifices it will take to succeed as a trader. As I will outline below, you need the capital, support from the family, and the discipline to come into every trading day with the proper perspective on where the current markets are and what gauges you need to watch for. Because there's no back-up salary in the event you mess up, your success depends on you and you alone. One last thing to know is that trading for a living is as hard a job as you could possibly choose. I've seen studies that claim only 10% of those who attempt to trade full time can consistently stay in the business. These odds are not good because many people are not mentally and fiscally prepared for the journey they are about to embark on.

# Paul's Strategies for a Trading Day

One of the questions I used to get often when I was trading full time was "Don't you get bored being home all the time and just sitting there trading?" The answer is YES! Fortunately, with the Internet and all its entertainment options, the boredom of sitting at home staring at a computer screen all day isn't as bad as it could be.

That's a good thing because when traders get bored, they sometimes can get sloppy. They end up trading for a little more action and often begin to raise the size of the share lots they buy. Many make the mistake of trying to become overly precise with their stock picking, and then rather than picking up 100 shares here or 200 there of a position, they go for the "perfect trade." This means they try to call the exact top or bottom of a stock when making a buy or sell. Bad move! When traders get sucked into this pattern, they see their investing returns begin to fall off.

If you want to trade for a living, you need to find your own comfort level for share lot sizes. Whenever I bought stock in 1,000-share lots, I noticed my performance numbers dropped significantly. Instead of buying 3–4 stocks, I'd put it all on one stock. This was the beginning of a horrible cycle of underperformance. I'd make my large purchase but still watch the other three stocks I was considering. When one of those other three stocks began to ramp up, my bulk position would drip down. I'd start getting antsy, and two hours later, I'd wind up getting out of my original position and into the one that was moving. When that stock began to drop, I'd get frustrated and sell out of that one. You can see the pattern developing here: Chasing stocks up with big positions is a recipe for disaster.

The best success I had in trading came from taking smaller positions, and when the stock I watched dropped 4% to 6%, but on lower volume, I would scale in and buy another 100 shares and then watch it more. I would usually carry 4–5 different positions and then look to pick up more when they were acting the way I expected. I always kept a stop-loss order in, usually at a 12% to 15% level drop in trade value (long or short). That was my "say goodbye" point, my comfort level. To use a baseball analogy, I would describe myself as a singles and doubles hitter when it came to trading. Leave the big "home run" swings for the Mutual Fund and Hedge Fund guys—they have lots of other people's capital to play with!

All investors needs to find their comfort zone, but scaling in slowly makes the most sense when you see a name you like. Let's take a look at an example. Say you are eyeing anywhere from 5–10 stocks on your radar. You have the capital to buy 500 shares of the best 3 or 4 names, but the smart way to begin is to decide what your first position size should be; I would use 100–150 shares as a good opening purchase. I would usually enter my orders when the market was already open for around an hour, because many times there are orders to buy at the market open that can make you pay a bit more than you really have to.

Usually the market settles down after the first 30–60 minutes of trading. Now, before I'd actually make my first purchase, I would check one key element that I feel is important. I like to see what price the stock has opened at and where it is trading when I am looking to buy the stock. This practice is important because sometimes the names you target may not be the best names to own, despite what your earlier research may have indicated.

Let's say my strategy was to buy stocks on my watch list that were trading above their opening price. This strategy would tell if the relative strength of these names was holding up and would usually eliminate some of the names from my earlier list. I now have my targets that I am ready to move ahead with. I would then enter my market orders and have my positions that I would monitor throughout the day. The, I'd only add to positions that were actually higher on the day, and not lower—this is contrary to what many traders may actually do on a daily basis. The reason I like to avoid buying names below the opening price is that there are many traders that normally do that. It's better to not be in this large crowd, and here's why: Investors tend to reassure themselves when they own positions by adding to losing positions. In a bull market, you are usually bailed out when the markets continue to run higher, so it's not really an issue. Where you run into a problem is when we are in a flat or bear market. Traders tend to get frustrated and eventually panic out of a position, usually selling into the lows of the day—so you are stuck in some tough company there.

You will hear the term "relative strength" a lot when investors talk about how well a stock is trading in relation to other stocks. Stocks with strong relative strength are usually the best names for investors to own, as long as the stocks are not over-extended. Over-extended stocks are those that are up more than 4–5 days in a row. You should also be wary of names that are trading 50% to 100% over their 50-day moving averages. These types of names tend to be called "momentum" stocks, and they can be extremely profitable. However, you must have good timing to avoid getting in near the top of a stock's run. Stocks that are near new highs tend to attract buyers, and there is no ceiling of sellers above that await them. In a flat-to-bear market you have to be quicker with taking profits than you'd normally be used to. This is one of the reasons why making money on a consistent basis on in the stock markets can prove difficult for many. Most investors do not like to change their routines, especially when theirs plans have been working for a period of time.

Navigating through the markets is similar to being on a cruise for the first time. I remember being on a cruise ship for the first time on my honeymoon. A friend advised me not fight the movement of the ship when moving around inside. Easier said that done, as human nature is to grab on to something or brace yourself for any odd movements. I noticed at first I was trying to keep myself still, but whenever I did, I'd start to feel a bit seasick. When I learned to go with the movements and flows of the ship, I was having a much better time and nothing seemed to bother me anymore. The same strategy applies to trading in the markets. If you start fighting the trend and flow of the markets, you will soon begin feeling the negative effects. You'll begin piling up losses instead of racking up wins. Don't ever fight the trend!

Let's get back to how I scale into positions. After making some initial buys, I would monitor the names I had purchased and watched to see how well they were holding up. If the stocks appeared to be gaining strength I would usually add my second amount of capital to the position (First purchase: 150 shares, second purchase: 150 shares). That second round of buying would usually carry me toward the last hour of trading, which is probably the most important hour of the trading day. Many times, the last hour of trading can determine how well the market will open the following day. In my many years of trading, I noticed that a high percentage of stocks that closed the day strong would likely open the next day strong as well. So, during the last hour, I'd look at my positions to see which were holding up well. If one of the three positions I owned was down just a little, that was no big deal, and I would usually hold on to it—but not add to the position at the close. If the other two were doing well, I would likely add the rest of my share purchase allocation to round out my objective as far as position size was concerned. So I would enter my last position, usually in the last ten minutes of trading, and again it would be a market order—before the market closes. So my allocation would look like this:

- First stock positions purchased usually by 10:30 a.m. (150 shares)
- Second position purchased after lunch, between 1:30 p.m.–2:15 p.m. (150 shares)
- Last positions purchased by 3:45–3:50 p.m. (200 shares)

If all three were working higher, the preceding scenario would happen with all of them. However, if two of my positions were flat for much of the day, I would not add to the positions at all but hold the original 150 shares into the next day to see if the stocks would begin to trade better. If any of the three stocks were down a bit, usually $1 at least, I would consider cutting the position off and looking at the stock again the next day. When it comes to the wash-sale rules, I don't worry about them because I would rather pay the taxes and get back in a stock before the 30 days go by, if the stock looks like it is ready to run. I would normally take a good share of wash-sale losses and get back in the names before 30 days would go by, if I felt the risk/reward made sense. Let's look at an example of this practice.

Let's say I liked Stock XYZ and purchased 500 shares at a cost of $14.50 per share. Now imagine the trade hasn't worked out, and I've had to sell the stock $1 lower. I now have a loss of $500 plus the commission costs. In a wash-sale rule situation, for me to write off the $500 plus loss, I would need to wait 30 days before I can buy the stock back to gain that tax advantage. What may occasionally happen is that one or more of the stocks you like may be mistimed, but not by much. You may take a loss, but you are still watching the name closely, because your research indicates it will move higher soon. Getting back to our example, let's say two days go by and XYZ is starting to act like you thought it would. You then have to decide whether you should get back in and not worry about the potential tax write-off gained from the first loss you took on the name, or if the risk/reward just doesn't make sense for you to get back in. If I feel I can make 4 points back in the name, I would likely take my shot and get back into it. Just make a note highlighting that the first $500 loss was a wash-sale violation, and you can not claim the loss of your capital gains. You need to keep good records of these types of trades because the IRS does monitor your accounts.

Risk/reward is another common term you will hear many top market strategists, investors, and traders use often. Risk/reward simply refers to the potential upside and downside for a stock's share price. I like to look at different variables to determine what I feel is the stocks' risk/reward. One of my favorite things to do is to see where the stocks have traded the previous 5–10 days, checking the range of the stock price. This practice is easy to do; simply visit Yahoo! Finance or Google Finance and enter the symbol for the stock you are researching. Go to the one month chart for the stock, and look at the last two weeks; you can get a good sense of what direction the stocks is currently in. One of the best places to look for profits in a bull market is buying stocks having mini-corrections in their uptrend. Let's say a stock that has been consistently hitting new highs is in the midst of a pullback. Depending on how far the stock has run, you can likely be a buyer in the down 15% from its 52-week high range. When you look at stocks that have been big winners over the last 52 weeks (up 40% or more is a big winner in my book), it is wise to pull up a 3-month chart to take a look at what the run has looked like. The one thing you have to be a bit careful about is chasing after stocks that go anywhere from 50% to 100% above their 50-day moving average. You can sometimes get caught in some fast pullbacks that you can see lose 3–4 points in the matter of just a few hours.

Even successful traders have periods of time in which they take on more losing trades than winning ones. The difference between a successful investor and one that is not so successful comes down to the willingness to take losses. I don't mind a scenario where I make 3 winning trades that net me $1,000 and 6 trades that lose me $600. In that case, I am still up $400 when all is said and done. On the flip-side there are many investors that will have 6 winning trades that make them $800 but then have two losing ones that cost then $1,200. The net total there is a $400 loss. I have said it before and I'll say it again: You will usually see the best traders are the ones that take the most losses.

**The Bottom Line** is to begin each day with a plan and a strategy for how you'll allocate your capital. This can determine whether you have profitable results or are just spinning your wheels. The above strategies are just some of many things you can take away from this book in helping you become a successful market investor or trader.

# Don't Let Taxes Affect How You Invest

New investors often ask about the effects of taxes on stock trading. We all know short-term capital gains taxes can be high, but for the type of work trading is, there are still not many other professions that can give you the ability to make a lot of money from the comfort of your home (or wherever else you want to trade from). You are basically in charge of your own personal business—only there aren't any customers to take care of.

I always tell investors to avoid letting tax concerns affect any part of your day-to-day strategy. Whether it means taking losses and maybe taking more wash-sales than you actually like to, or sitting on a stock beginning to break down that has several month-long runs but is still not at the one-year threshold for long-term capital gains tax benefits to kick in, don't let the tax implications of any trade dictate your course of action. Accountants tend to over-magnify tax situations when it comes to trading, so be sure you have an accountant that understands what it is you do and what the tax implications are for someone considered a full-time trader. There are also programs you can run to help manage your trading data that can make it easier for your accountant to use. Ask your accountant what products she is comfortable with. Your accounting charge may be higher as well because more work is usually involved but don't sweat the small stuff if you find someone you are comfortable with.

**The Bottom Line** is you will encounter many situations during the course of the stock market that will affect how long you hold positions for. If you're a trader, stick to trading, and leave the taxes to your accountant. Otherwise, you risk compromising your trading strategy.

# If You Want to Sleep at Night, Don't Play the "Earnings Game"

I noticed early in my trading career that I seemed to make more mistakes when I bought and sold stocks during small windows of time. Ask any trader who will probably tell you that the opening bell is perhaps the biggest adrenaline moment that a trader can endure. Some will argue, however, that the biggest emotional rush happens *after* the bell when a company releases its earnings report. There is almost always some stock news that moves certain names, whether it's an analyst ratings change or earnings news, or even possible merger and acquisition news. Nothing can make a trader more excited than knowing that a stock may be ready to take off, and you need to decide whether it pays to chase a stock up after the train has already left the station. The same applies when a stock moves down; you need to decide whether to depart the stock.

I realized that my biggest losses would come in the mornings when I would buy stocks at the open because I feared that the stock would get away from me, and I'd miss out on potential gains. Fortunately, I learned to avoid this practice early on and corrected the situation quickly. The urge to jump on names early still remained, however, so instead I learned to take smaller positions early in the day to "taste" the stock and make sure the early move up or down was not what athletes would call a "head fake," or a false signal.

During my early years of trading, I also bore witness to the "earnings game" at the height of its popularity. The earnings game—where traders place bets on big stock moves based on expectations of good or bad after-hours earnings reports—is still quite active today but not nearly to the degree I had witnessed in my earlier years. Anyone that was in the markets in the late 90s can recount the days in which

America Online (AOL) would report, beat the earnings estimates, jump up, announce a split, and jump up even more. Dell Computer (DELL), Cisco Systems (CSCO), and Microsoft (MSFT) were also prominent names that would reward those that got into the earnings game. In the earnings game strategy, traders buy the shares either the week before or the same week of the earnings report and then sell the shares the following day after the stocks would open up with a big spike. For many names back then, it was like printing money. Unfortunately, the game spread to weaker names as well, and sometimes the results were disastrous.

I remember one instance in the early 2000s when a company called Analog Devices (ADI) was set to report its quarterly earnings, and I was confident by looking at previous earnings report reactions that the stock would usually rally nicely after it reported. I was ready to go, and my emotions were at a high. I remember taking a 2,000-share position and salivating about how much money I would be banking the following day. The company reported a good number after the bell, and I was ecstatic. But then sometime strange happened.

The company began its customary conference call, and management decided they were going to rein in some of the company's guidance for the next quarter. The stock was halted and did not trade after hours. Let's just say that was an uncomfortable night of sleep for me! It was one of the few restless nights I'd ever had during my full-time tenure as a trader. Remember, I was used to being on the right side of the trade for the majority of the time, and that was partially due to the big bull market we were in but also due to my rigorous research.

Anyway, the next morning, as the stock was set to open, I flipped on the TV and saw a CNBC analyst standing on the trading floor saying that my stock was indicated down nearly 5 points. This was a huge reality check for me as a trader and also coincided with the top of the technology stocks' run. I had to decide whether I thought the stock would open and bounce back up or to just cut my losses right then and there. Disregarding my emotions, I decided to place a market order as the stock was opening and let the position go. I was a bit fortunate in that the stock filled about a dollar off the early indication lows (meaning the price I was able to actually sell at was higher than originally indicated), but I still ended up losing a significant amount of money in that one trade.

**The Bottom Line** is that one single bad trade changed the way I looked at the earnings game. Shortly thereafter, I spoke to trader friends of mine and told them that I felt the market climate was changing and that many of the high-flying companies were beginning to send us a different message than we were used to. My friends felt I had simply let one bad trade throw me off course, but I stuck to my guns and remembered watching many tech companies disappoint investors in the following months. Thousands of investors began to get hurt by the earnings game, and instead of exercising discipline like I did, many let their emotions run wild. Some of my trader friends began to get careless by "doubling down" on stocks they owned that would open down, only to see the stocks not bounce at all, turning $2,000–$3,000 losses into $10,000–$15,000 losses by days' end. Eventually, all the traders I knew personally were knocked out of the trading game for good.

# How 9/11 Affected My Trading

There are some things in life that we can never be truly prepared for. Leading up to the horrific events of 9/11, I remember the markets were not performing very well, and I seemed to be making a lot more trades than I usually had. That was a bad sign in my own trading mind because I seemed to be making a couple of hundred dollars in the morning and then losing $150 in the afternoon. That was the sort of pattern I fell into at the time, and vice versa, losing in the morning and profiting late in the day. The only thing I felt I was doing right back in the fall of 2001 was that I kept my positions small. Whenever you are unsure about the markets but feel the need to be trading, do yourself a favor and keep your position size small (100–500 shares per transaction).

The entire year of 2001 seemed to be like that for me. The summer was no fun trading, and at the time I hadn't started short-selling yet, so I could only make money in "up" markets. I timed many of my trades and would love to pick up momentum stocks after they dropped for a couple of days. I remember going into September thinking that there was no edge at all and the markets were uneventful. Mergers and acquisitions activity was quiet, and the economy was lethargic. I was getting into a habit of closing out all my positions on Friday and starting fresh on Monday. Luckily, I had no positions going into the morning of 9/11, unlike many of my trading colleagues who were usually in fully invested positions that would carry over through the weekend.

The markets were still prepared to open that morning after the first plane crashed into the World Trade Center, but when the second plane crashed, the powers that be decided against it. There would be no trading that day, nor for the rest of the week. As that horrifying week was nearing an end, the inevitable question on investors' minds became "How much will the markets drop?" Many fellow traders were telling me that I was lucky I had no open positions. Truly, sometimes in life and in business, we are more lucky than smart.

My advice to traders back then was to create a plan of action and execute it. Panicking will never make you money, but at a time like that, there was no way of knowing how things would play out when the markets eventually reopened. I didn't trade much during the first few market days after 9/11, but I did eventually get back into the markets. When I did start trading again, I didn't hold any stocks at the end of each day. I was totally off my game that year, and my performance, though still profitable, was the worst year I ever had as a trader. I stopped carrying positions through to the next day, which had been one of my favorite things to do during the week. Before 9/11, I loved buying stocks that closed strong and would open stronger the following day. I eventually made a vow at the end of the year that I needed to get back to the basics and accept holding positions at the end of the day. Plus, I dedicated myself to learning the art of short-selling which we'll cover in the next section.

**The Bottom Line** is that 9/11 changed the markets drastically, and my style needed to be enhanced to compensate. No more being a one-punch fighter (making money mostly only on up days). I needed to learn the jab (short-selling). For long-term investors, this may not be as important, but for those that like to look at short-term plays, I believe the ability to make money going long and short should be something any trader investor should strive for.

## Shorting Is a Good Weapon to Possess When Needed

As I said, learning to short sell was a goal I had at the end of 2001. The markets were not performing well, so I figured I needed to embrace that part of the market and add short selling to my trading arsenal. Whenever you try something new in investing, remember to start small. Some people like to paper trade (virtual trading with fake money), but in my experience, paper trading simply doesn't emulate the process of putting actual money to work. Do professional poker players play their normal game at holiday gatherings with Uncle Joe and Aunt Dottie when the prize is a mere $20 buy-in for each player? Probably not. Most probably play much looser and therefore don't perform as well as they do when real money is at stake.

When I first started to short stocks, I'd look at names that I felt were overextended and add some small shorts on the books (my trading account). It worked for the most part, except when stocks that were extended became more extended. By 2004, this phenomenon took hold, and my shorting strategy needed some tweaking. It was then that I realized the best shorts were in the sectors that were performing the worst. The beauty of that strategy really kicks in at the end of fiscal quarters and fiscal years, when fund managers want to make sure the losers are gone from their holdings. Guess what happens then: The losers go down even more.

A word of caution: Shorting stocks can be difficult in an environment in which there are a lot of mergers and acquisitions taking place. In these environments, short-sellers can wake up to find the stocks they bet against being taken over for a big premium. This is a true short-seller's nightmare! In the dot-com boom of the late 1990s, many short-sellers were eventually proven right for their bearishness. Unfortunately, most were not around to collect when the drop finally came because they were nursing some of the largest losses ever recorded in trading histories.

Attempting to short-sell in a bull market can be one of the worst moves an investor can ever make. Trying to "call a top" during investing manias more often than not will lead to financial suicide. During any buying frenzy, it is better to simply get out of the way if you are not along for the ride up. In general, you should stick to shorting the weakest sectors and get out when the merger players come in—and the stocks stop going down on bad news.

In the summer of 2008, just as my Dividend.com DARS™ rating system had debuted, I made what some had felt was a controversial call advising investors that a top in the energy and commodity sectors had formed. Take a look at a post I wrote July 19, 2008, about some of the hottest coal stock plays that had been ripping higher over the last few years.

> Coal stocks have given investors a spectacular run the last five years. We think it's time for investors to use the rallies now to think about lightening up their positions. Look at the gains for some of the names based on recent highs they hit in recent weeks.
>
> • Walter Industries (WLT) stock is up 1200%—Dividend yield is now .22%.

- Massey Energy (MEE) stock is up 800%—Dividend yield is now .30%.

- Peabody Energy (BTU) stock is up 1,200%—Dividend yield is now .37%.

- Arch Coal (ACI) stock is up 700%—Dividend yield is now .53%.

- Consol Energy (CNX) stock is up 1,200%—Dividend yield is now .49%.

The stocks have now begun to have a fairly decent-sized correction. It's one that we think will bounce up this week, but we believe that will be an opportunity to trim some of those gains. We saw a deal this week to buy Alpha Natural Resources (ANR) that failed to lift the sector, and that was something that we feel may be an omen for the coal sector. We have started to take some coal names (ACI, CNX) off the "Recommended" list this past week, and if our research is right, there will be more coal plays following them off the list.

For investors, the hardest thing to do is to sell stocks that have treated your portfolio as well as these coal stocks have done. One of the things to remember is that often times, the best time to buy stocks is when nobody likes them. Eight years ago, coal stocks were in the dumps and investors were printing money with Internet stock profits. We all know how that ended. The energy crisis is not over by any means, but with the backlash we have seen in the media aimed at energy executives and the sky-high price of oil and gas, we think the consumer is starting to be pro-active when it comes to conserving energy. (Dealers can't sell hybrids fast enough.) The dividend yields [just]shown) will not support investors with any decent-sized drop in stock price from these levels. Combine that with the slowdown we are seeing in economies worldwide, and we think the rotation out of coal stocks, as well as other energy sectors may have started.

By the end of the year, most of the preceding stocks had fallen between 50% and 80% from their highs. I fielded plenty of emails at the time of publishing that article, however, claiming that I didn't know what I was talking about. Many investors still felt the energy, coal, and steel plays had plenty of fuel left to keep firing upward. My response was subtle, and I basically said that taking something off the table would not have been a bad thing to do, and for those that never used a stop-loss, this would be a good time for many to learn how to implement that particular stock trading tool.

**The Bottom Line** is that short-selling is a great tool to have in your trading arsenal because it enables you the chance to make money in down markets. The energy, coal, and steel stocks I mentioned above presented traders with one of the best short-selling opportunities of all time. The key to identifying these sorts of situations is to watch the best-performing sectors closely and wait for signs of the inevitable correction.

# The Dangers of Short-Selling

Back in late 2002, I was in the midst of using my newest investing tool: short-selling. I was cleaning up on the short side, and I started focusing exclusively on the short side of the markets, where I felt the best opportunities were. Yahoo! (YHOO) was about to report its quarterly earnings, and I was up nicely on the year, so I decided to press my luck and got my short position up to 6,000 shares. (At the time, Yahoo was about $9.30 per share.) The company was struggling, and Internet stocks in general barely had a pulse. I did my homework, the analysts were expecting a loss, and there was not much hope for surprise on the upside. Yahoo's earnings report came out, and as expected, the news was not good. I nailed it! I couldn't wait to watch the share price implode, but much to my disbelief, the price was slightly unchanged. I went to the store and figured tomorrow the downgrades would hit the company, and I'd be able to cash in my position then. The next day, Yahoo stock rose to over $10.50, despite several analyst downgrades and lowered price targets. As the trading day came, I planned on watching the stock drip down, and was actually considering shorting more shares. Fortunately, I didn't. The stock closed near $11, and I was stunned.

Everything I expected happened, except for the most important thing: The stock didn't go down! The next day, as the stock approached $11.50, I began to realize that it was not going to drop down to where I had hoped. I covered my position, and took a big loss. The Trading Gods had taken a big chunk out of my year-to-date gains. I still ended the year well but what a piece of humble pie I ate.

Within one month after that, Yahoo's stock hit $15. Shortly thereafter, it rose to $20, $30, and eventually $42. I used to add up the potential losses, imagining I had held my convictions and never covered. That Yahoo trade still goes down to this day as the biggest loss I've ever had.

**The Bottom Line** is to make sure you stay disciplined and cover your shorts on stocks when they stop going down on bad news!

# Check Your Brokerage Account for Mistakes Periodically

Investors sometimes take their brokerage account for granted. In the midst of a trading year, you'll likely engage in numerous transactions, and that means more possibility for error. The key is checking your account periodically so that you catch any mistakes quickly. I've been guilty myself of assuming I've completed every transaction correctly. A common mistake is to enter an order, make sure it gets filled, and then lazily forget to check to see if it were the correct order type you want. For example, let's say that I was looking to close out a 300-share position and I put in my "sell" order to sell the 300 shares. I enter the order and then make sure it was filled but don't pay attention to whether I hit the Sell choice. It's entirely possible I could have hit the Buy button by mistake—and accidentally added to my position instead of liquidating it.

Anyone who has traded often can tell you that mistakes happen more often than you think. Do yourself a favor and set up a routine where you check your holdings either every day you make a transaction or once a week to at least monitor any suspicious activity in your account. You may be the victim of a hacker who has obtained your password and can possibly have access to your brokerage funds. Don't take things, such as checking your account on a regular basis, for granted.

**The Bottom Line** is that it's easy to forget the simple task of periodically looking at your holdings to make sure everything in your account is in tip-top shape. It takes only a minute and is well worth the time.

# Conclusion

I hope this book can be a valuable tool to help any investor get started in the markets, or even as a refresher to help refocus your investing efforts. I have enjoyed a successful career navigating the markets and have consistently found situations that helped me build up my personal worth. Now, I am excited at the chance to take my investing success and share my knowledge via this book to help people build their own nest eggs with a focus on dividend stock investing. I truly believe that dividends will continue to outperform many investment vehicles, and I take great pride in being the "catalyst" for investors who want to follow the proprietary Dividend Advantage Ratings System (DARS) that I have developed.

Good luck with your investing, and be sure to keep this book handy. I hope this book becomes something you can pass down for generations to come because much of its content will likely remain relevant for investors and traders for several decades. Finally, I want to thank everyone that has been there along the way for my journey, especially my family, colleagues, and friends who have believed in me and what I have aspired to achieve.

# INDEX